# SKY'S THE LIMIT

## A Farcical Comedy in Three Acts

by

ARNOLD HELSBY

LONDON

SAMUEL FRENCH LIMITED

**SAMUEL FRENCH LTD**
26 SOUTHAMPTON STREET, STRAND, LONDON, W.C.2

**SAMUEL FRENCH INC.**
25 WEST 45TH STREET, NEW YORK, U.S.A.
7623 SUNSET BOULEVARD, HOLLYWOOD 46, CAL.

**SAMUEL FRENCH (CANADA) LTD**
27 GRENVILLE STREET, TORONTO

**SAMUEL FRENCH (AUSTRALIA) PTY LTD**
159 FORBES STREET, SYDNEY

822

MADE AND PRINTED IN GREAT BRITAIN BY
LATIMER, TREND AND CO., LTD, PLYMOUTH

MADE IN ENGLAND

# CHARACTERS

*(in the order of their appearance)*

CHARLIE GIBBS, Fred's rival
WILLIE WATSON, apprentice to Charlie
EMMA DERBYSHIRE, Fred's sister-in-law
GLADYS FURNIVAL, Fred's wife
JOE DERBYSHIRE, Fred's brother-in-law
PETER GIBBS, Charlie's son
CISSIE FURNIVAL, Fred's daughter
FRED FURNIVAL
JIM DOBSON, a policeman
MRS WATSON, Willie's mother
A CURATE

## SYNOPSIS OF SCENES

*The action of the play passes in the living-room of the Furnivals' house in Prestfield*

### ACT I

Friday night

### ACT II

Early Saturday morning

### ACT III

The following Thursday

*Time—the present*

# SKY'S THE LIMIT

## ACT I

SCENE—*The living-room of the Furnival home in Prestfield, one Friday night.*

*The room is in the process of decoration and the furniture is covered with dust sheets. The flats on the left-hand side of the stage are already covered with the new wallpaper but those on the right are covered with the old. A note on how this is devised will be found at the end of the play. Back C there is a box window from which the curtains have been stripped. Up L is a door at an angle which leads to the hall and front door; up R is a flight of stairs leading to a landing and the bedrooms; R of the stairs is a door leading to the kitchen and the back door. The fireplace is R. Beneath the window stands a pasting-board on trestles which holds the painter's paraphanalia; up C there is a gate-legged table with four bent-wood chairs standing R and L and above it. There is a settee L and an armchair R; down R there is a pouffe. The sideboard stands L against the wall. A stag's head is fixed to the wall above the fireplace; suitable dressing may be added to the set at the discretion of the producer.*

*(See the Ground Plan at the end of the Play)*

*When the* CURTAIN *rises the table and four chairs are stacked against the settee.* CHARLIE GIBBS *is standing on a painter's ladders putting the finishing touches to a length of wallpaper he has just hung on the back wall up L.* WILLIE WATSON, *the apprentice, is sitting in the armchair R deeply immersed in a comic.* CHARLIE *steps down with his back to the audience and surveys his work.*

CHARLIE. Well—that's it for tonight. (*He picks up the paste bucket and stirs*) This paste's thick! What did you mix it with?

(*There is no reply*)

CHARLIE (*still with his back to the audience*) Willie!!
WILLIE (*half-hearing*) Mm?
CHARLIE. What did you mix this paste with?
WILLIE. Blood!
CHARLIE (*dropping the bucket and turning round*) *Blood!* Where from?
WILLIE (*reading*) "Under the door—a thick pool staining the carpet. Suddenly a voice screamed out: 'Help—my throat! It's cut!'"
CHARLIE (*moving down R*) And your backside'll be kicked in a

minute! What do you think I pay you for? Give it to me! (*Taking the comic*) And get these sheets off! If we're not out of here before Fred Furnival gets home—there'll be 'ell to pay!

(*During the next few speeches,* WILLIE *and* CHARLIE, *having removed the dust sheet over the table and the bentwood chairs, return them to their normal positions up* C, *as they converse*)

WILLIE. You don't like him, do you?
CHARLIE. No.
WILLIE. *He* doesn't like you?
CHARLIE. No.
WILLIE. Why not?
CHARLIE. What's it got to do with you?
WILLIE. Well, you told me if there was anything I didn't know I'd got to ask.
CHARLIE. About decorating—yes. But not my private life! Surely you don't expect me to tell you the last time I had a bath?
WILLIE. Can't you remember?
CHARLIE (*dropping a chair*) One more bit o' cheek out of you, my lad . . .
WILLIE. All right, Mister Gibbs—I'm sorry.
CHARLIE. I should think so!
WILLIE (*moving* R) I thought you said we'd finish this job tonight?
CHARLIE. So we should have done. And goodness knows what Gladys Furnival 'ull say when she sees it's only half finished. What's more I don't intend to be here to find out. Give me my jacket!

(CHARLIE *crosses to the armchair* R *as he removes his white painter's coat.* WILLIE *picks up Charlie's jacket which is lying over the back of the armchair and hands it to him, receiving the white coat in return.* CHARLIE *starts to put on his jacket with his back to the door* L.
EMMA DERBYSHIRE *enters* L *carrying numerous parcels. She turns and closes the door without seeing Charlie*)

EMMA (*calling*) I'm back, Gladys!
CHARLIE (*turning*) Shush!
EMMA. Charlie Gibbs! (*She drops her parcels in surprise*)
CHARLIE (*turning down* C) Be quiet, woman!

(WILLIE *now begins unobtrusively to remove the dust sheets from the rest of the furniture and stack them against the back wall up* R. *He places Charlie's white coat over the back of the settee which is now clear and the ladders up* R *with the dust sheets. He pushes the trestle table against the wall under the window and the paste bucket under the* L *end*)

EMMA. What are you doing here?

CHARLIE. If it comes to that, Emma Derbyshire—what are *you* doing here?

(EMMA *picks up her parcels*)

EMMA. Didn't you know? I'm living here. (*She puts the parcels on the upstage end of the settee*)

CHARLIE. Living here?

EMMA. Yes. Me and Joe. It's only temporary like—till they've repaired the damage at our house.

CHARLIE. What damage?

EMMA. Subsidence—it's disturbed the foundations.

CHARLIE. Is it bad?

EMMA. Bad? It's got that many timbers propping it up—Joe says if anyone breaks a bottle of champagne on it—they'll launch it!

CHARLIE. So you're living here with your sister? Bit crowded, aren't you?

EMMA. Well, Joe being a night-watchman—he's only in days. And now the old lady's taken bad—I'm only in nights.

CHARLIE. The old lady! Is your mother still alive?

EMMA. Eighty next month—and still living on her own. But when she's not so grand it means somebody being with her all day.

CHARLIE. What about nights?

EMMA. Gladys sleeps there. That reminds me—she should be on her way—it's gone nine! Where is she?

CHARLIE (*pointing*) Upstairs. She went early on. Said she'd got a headache.

EMMA. I hope it's better then.

CHARLIE. If it's not—she'll have *two* when she comes down!

WILLIE (*at the back of the settee*) Can I go now, Mister Gibbs?

CHARLIE. Yes—'op it! (*He moves up* L *to Willie*) And don't forget—eight o'clock sharp in the morning!

WILLIE (*over at the door* L) O.K.! I'll make it five-past—then I shan't have to wait for you! Ta-ta!

(WILLIE *exits* L)

EMMA (*moving to the fireplace*) Does Fred know you're here?

CHARLIE (*moving down* C *to Emma*) Not yet. And when he does —you keep your eye on that stag's head. (*He points to it*)

EMMA. What for?

CHARLIE. When it hears his language—it'll shove its horns in it's ear-holes!

EMMA. Here! You be careful what you say about that head. That's not Fred's!

CHARLIE. It'd suit him better than the one he's got!

EMMA. It belongs to me, that does. The only thing Joe and I brought with us apart from clothing.

CHARLIE. But why bring it here?

EMMA. Because it's our lucky mascot—(*speaking to it*) aren't you, Lulu?

CHARLIE (*aghast*) Lulu! You don't mean to say you call that thing *Lulu?*

EMMA. Why not?

CHARLIE. It's a girl's name!

EMMA. I know it is.

CHARLIE. But just look at them horns!

EMMA (*coldly*) Mr Gibbs! Nature may have supplied the head— but kindly allow me to provide my own body!

CHARLIE. Well, I shouldn't stick the body on—or there'll be a rum view next door! (*He jerks his thumb towards the kitchen*)

EMMA. You haven't changed a bit, Charlie. Still as coarse as ever! And to think our Gladys might have married you.

CHARLIE. Aye. She had the chance. Two years we were walking out. And now look what she's got!

EMMA. Fred?

CHARLIE (*leaning back against the table; scornfully*) Fred Furnival! Lovey-dovey, pie-eyed, butter-won't-melt-in-my-mouth Fred Furnival!

EMMA. You must admit one thing. He's a better breeder and fancier than you.

CHARLIE. With one difference. *I* breed and fancy pigeons!

EMMA. And what about Fred?

CHARLIE. He breeds trouble—and fancies himself!

EMMA (*indicating the decorating*) Well, he'll certainly breed trouble about this. He can't put up with that son of yours—never mind you!

CHARLIE. Our Peter? Does he come here?

EMMA. So that's something else you don't know?

CHARLIE. Here—what are you getting at?

EMMA. You courted the mother—why shouldn't he have an eye for the daughter?

CHARLIE. Look—if you've any match-making ideas for my Peter—you can count Fred Furnival's girl right out of it. Why dammit—I'd sooner he married Lulu! (*He points to the stag's head*)

EMMA. Don't be vulgar!

CHARLIE. Anyway, if there has been any romancin' between 'em—you can take it from me—it's finished!

GLADYS (*off; from the stairs*) It ought to have been finished hours ago! Off you go before Fred gets in!

CHARLIE (*indicating to Emma to keep quiet, and moving towards the door* L) Right-oh, Glad! Ta-ta, Emma!

> (CHARLIE *exits* L *closing the door.*
> GLADYS *appears at the top of the stairs* R *carrying a tea-tray*)

GLADYS (*descending*) Well, Emma—how's Ma today?

EMMA (*moving to the fireplace*) About the same. I must say this is a surprise.

GLADYS (*moving behind the table, depositing the tray on it and looking with admiration towards the wall* L) You like it?

EMMA. It'll be nice when it's finished.

GLADYS. When it's *finished?* (*She turns and sees the wall* R. *Her mouth opens in astonishment, and then closes resolutely*) *Where* is he?

(EMMA *nods towards the door* L)

GLADYS (*calling*) Charlie! (*She rushes over to the door* L *and flings it open*)

(CHARLIE *steps in and stands there shamefacedly fingering his cap*)

CHARLIE. Did somebody shout "Charlie"?

GLADYS (*moving down* C *in front of the table*) Somebody *did!* Come in and shut that door.

CHARLIE. Listen, Glad . . . (*He moves to the upstage end of the settee*)

GLADYS. Don't tell me! I've heard too many lies already. (*Mimicking*) "Oh yes, Glad—I'll do it in a day—long before Fred gets home—best paper-hanger in Prestfield, that's me!"

EMMA (*protesting*) But he is the best . . .

GLADYS. Hang paper? Him! He can't hang his trousers over a bed-rail!

CHARLIE (*protesting*) It's not my fault. I would have finished but for Mrs Cripps!

GLADYS. What's she got to do with it?

CHARLIE. She came just after you'd gone upstairs. Made me go round to her house to have a look at something in the kitchen.

GLADYS. What?

CHARLIE. Her belly.

EMMA } (*together*) *What!*
GLADYS }

CHARLIE. Belly! In the ceiling paper. (*He points upwards*) I just had to put it right, Glad. Strip it all off and paste it on again.

EMMA. Couldn't it have waited?

CHARLIE. Listen, Emma—if you'd seen that poor old woman crawling on her hands and knees across the kitchen with a shovelful of coal . . .

GLADYS. But what am I going to tell Fred?

CHARLIE. Don't worry. As soon as he's gone to work in the morning, I'll be in and finish it.

EMMA. Are you forgetting what tomorrow is?

CHARLIE. It's Saturday—and Fred works Saturdays.

EMMA. Not tomorrow! He starts his annual holiday.

CHARLIE. Am I not to turn up in the morning then?

GLADYS. No. You'd better wait till you hear from me.

CHARLIE (*moving towards the door* L) As you will! Anyway, good

luck with him, Gladys. (*Turning at the open door*) And don't forget
—if the worst comes to the worst . . .

GLADYS. Well?

CHARLIE. You can always apply for police protection. Ta-ta!

(CHARLIE *exits* L *closing the door*)

GLADYS. What a fool of a man he is! (*She moves up* LC)

EMMA (*moving down* C) You didn't always think so. Do you
remember that foggy night when you helped him out of the
canal?

GLADYS. Yes. *And* I remember what I pushed him in for!

EMMA. Anyway, it was a big surprise finding him here. What
made you do it? (*She moves to the armchair* R)

GLADYS. Fred. (*She sits* C *of the settee*)

EMMA. I'm not having that! Fred hates him. (*She sits in the
armchair* R)

GLADYS. I mean Fred's idleness. I'm just sick to my heart of
his promises. Eighteen months he's been going to do this decorating. I've thrown hints out every day. And what did I get? "I'll
start next week—as soon as I've finished the garden"—"When
I've repaired the pigeon-shed". And then the night before last—
just when I thought I'd got him cornered—what do you think he
came out with?

EMMA. What?

GLADYS. "Will you rub my back, love? If I try to get my hands
above my head, it cripples me!"

EMMA. Was he pretending?

GLADYS. I don't know—but when he gets his hands in his
pockets to pay for this lot—we'll see if *that* cripples him?

(*The door* L *opens and* CISSIE *enters, followed by* PETER)

CISSIE (*crossing behind the table towards the fireplace*) Sorry I'm
late, Mum. Hello, Aunt Emma. Oh—I've brought Peter. He
wants to ask you something.

(CISSIE *gives her nose a dab of powder by the fireplace.* PETER *has
made his way nervously to the upstage end of the settee. There is a slight
pause*)

GLADYS. Well?

PETER (*nervously*) Er—how are you, Mrs Furnival—Mrs
Derbyshire?

(*There is another slight pause*)

GLADYS. Is that it?

CISSIE. What?

GLADYS. What he wanted to ask?

PETER. No, no. I wondered if you'd mind if I took Cissie to the
pictures?

GLADYS. At this time? You're a bit late, aren't you?

PETER. Not for the second feature. Besides we won't have to pay.

GLADYS. Why not?

PETER. The operator's a pal of mine. He says if I'll take Cissie up the fire escape . . .

GLADYS. Oh, no, you don't!

CISSIE. Why not?

GLADYS. He's not slinging you over his shoulder and climbing a ladder. Besides, if it's windy—it isn't decent!

CISSIE. Don't be silly. It's a proper staircase! (*She moves* C *towards Peter*) I see you've started the decorating? I'll bet Dad went crazy over it!

GLADYS. Not yet, love—you're about five minutes too soon! Now off you go before he arrives!

CISSIE (*moving to the door* L *with Peter*) All right, Mum. Good-bye.

PETER. Good-bye, Mrs Furnival.

(CISSIE *and* PETER *exit through the door* L)

EMMA (*rising and coming* C *to the front of the table*) I know it's none of my business—but do you think it's right letting Cissie knock about with him? After all he is Charlie Gibbs' son. And you know what Fred thinks.

GLADYS. Listen. I've spent twenty-five years of my married life wondering what Fred was thinking. Now it's his turn!

EMMA. What do you mean?

GLADYS. He can spend the next twenty-five wondering what I'm thinking!

EMMA. All the same—I still think this—(*she moves up* L *and indicates the decorating*)—is a bit drastic!

GLADYS. Drastic? (*She rises and crosses to the fireplace* R) It'll teach him a lesson! (*She picks up the slippers and re-positions them on the hearth*)

EMMA. I mean bringing Charlie Gibbs in. There's plenty of other decorators, surely?

GLADYS. None that I could get hold of at a minute's notice. And if only Charlie had kept his word—there was no need for Fred to know *who'd* done it.

EMMA. What about when he gets the bill?

GLADYS. Don't worry—Fred won't see that. *I'll* write his bill out—and I'll write it with thick ink!

FRED (*shouting off* L) All aboard! Gangway for a naval officer!

(*A bicycle bell rings violently*)

EMMA. You'd better get your pen out—he's here!

(*Sound of kicking on door* L)

FRED (*off*) Open this door somebody!

(EMMA *exits* L *leaving the door open.* GLADYS *crosses and sits on the downstage end of the settee.*

*A moment later* FRED FURNIVAL *enters* L; *he is wheeling a dilapidated bicycle with difficulty as he is balancing a bulky brown paper parcel on the handlebars, in his left hand he carries a pigeon-basket.*

EMMA *follows him and closes the door*)

FRED (*coming down* C) Well, here we are—I say here we are! Emma! Take this thing off me!

(EMMA *takes the bicycle and props it against the front of the table*)

FRED (*going over to the armchair* R *he puts a pigeon-basket behind the chair and a brown paper parcel on the floor to the* R *of the chair. He is so full of himself that he never notices the decorating*) Where's my tea? If it's ready—I don't want it! If it isn't—somebody had better get cracking! Emma! Take a letter! (*Pacing up and down like a big executive, holding the lapels of his coat*) "To the Managing Director—Peabody's Canning Factory—Dear Sir: This is to inform you that I shall not be present next week—it being my annual holiday. You can stick . . . a reply in the post. Yours, Fred Furnival". Where's my slippers?

GLADYS. Why don't you use 'your eyes?

FRED. Because I can't get 'em on my feet! Come on—*where's* my slippers?

GLADYS. They'll bite you if you're not careful!

FRED (*picking up his slippers from the hearth and feeling them*) They're not warm?

GLADYS. We've no fire.

FRED. Well, somebody could have worn them! (*He throws them down in disgust*)

(GLADYS *rises and crosses to the fireplace retrieving the slippers and placing them back in the hearth*)

FRED. All right. Let's hear the news. Who's dead? Who's had a baby? Who should have had one and hasn't? All right—who shouldn't have had a baby and has?

(EMMA *sits* C *of the settee.* GLADYS, *rising from the hearth, sniffs suspiciously*)

FRED. What are you sniffing for? You can smell something, can't you? Peppermint, isn't it? You can smell peppermint, can't you? *Can't you?* All right—get a load of this! (*Breathing out heavily*) Do you know what that is? That's the drop o' whisky I had to get rid of the peppermint! Well—what else is biting you?

GLADYS. You've no thought for me. None at all!

FRED. What have I done now?

GLADYS. That bicycle—wheeling it in here.

FRED. What do you want me to do—*ride it?*

GLADYS. You know very well . . .

FRED. And that reminds me. Who's pinched my pump? You know I've got a slow puncture.

GLADYS. I know nothing of the sort.

FRED. Anyway, let's not quarrel about it, because I've got a surprise for you. (*Bending down over the* R *arm of the chair and untying the string round the parcel*)

GLADYS. I've got one for you, too! (*She crosses in front of Fred and sits on the downstage end of the settee next to Emma*)

FRED (*still untying*) Not like mine. You know we can't go away next week?

GLADYS. Why not?

FRED (*straightening up again and looking at Gladys*) It's the big race. (*Smiling and staring out into space*) Oh—I can see my name on that cup now. "Won by Furnival Skyranger—bred by Fred Furnival, Esquire". Good old Sky! She'll win it hands down! (*Looking back at Gladys*) And because we're not going away—I've decided to do something for you.

GLADYS. For me? What?

FRED. The decorating. (*Bending to the parcel again*)

GLADYS (*aghast*) Decorating?

FRED. Yes. I'm going to paper this room. (*He takes a roll of wallpaper out of the parcel, rises, drapes a length over his arm and displays it*) Now—how do you like that?

(*It can be seen that the pattern is identical with the new paper on the wall* L)

FRED. Isn't that the one we fancied?

(GLADYS *and* EMMA *have both risen.* GLADYS *is standing petrified, hand to mouth.* EMMA *collects her parcels and starts moving towards the stairs*)

FRED. I thought you'd be surprised. (*He holds the piece against the faded paper on the wall* R, *with his back to Gladys*) Emma! Do you like it?

EMMA (*at the foot of the stairs*) It's—it's very nice.

FRED. Where are you going?

EMMA (*nervously*) I'd better see what's happened to Joe. He should have been down long ago.

(EMMA *exits hurriedly up the stairs*)

FRED (*still holding up the paper*) If you don't like it—I can always get it changed.

GLADYS (*quietly*) I think you'd better.

FRED. But I thought you said this would match the curtains and the carpet?

GLADYS. So it does. Have a look for yourself. (*She indicates the wall* L)

(FRED *turns and sees the newly-decorated half for the first time. For a moment he is bewildered. He stares at the wall, at the paper in his hands, and then the resentment and aggression build up. He throws out his chest, cocks his head to one side, and uses the roll of wallpaper as a pointer*)

FRED (*moving* C *towards Gladys*) What's going on behind my back? Why haven't I been told? Why didn't somebody say something? Why don't *you* say something? Go on—explain!

GLADYS. Well—I . . .

FRED (*jumping in*) That's a lie for a start! Did I say I'd decorate this room? Did I—or did I not?

GLADYS (*moving slightly* C *towards him*) I'm having this decorating done because I've waited eighteen months for you to do it—and as far as I could see I was likely to wait another eighteen!

FRED (*turning away down* R, *hurt*) So that's it! I don't keep my word!

GLADYS. Of course you don't!

FRED (*turning his back to her; sharply*) Give me an example. Go on—give me just one example!

GLADYS. All right! What about that cistern down the yard. How long's that been running over?

FRED. I've told you. It's the overflow. It's blocked up!

GLADYS. Yes—and it looks well, doesn't it—sending visitors down there in a mac' and a sou'wester?

FRED. Well—it's not wide enough for an umbrella! (*He turns slightly down* R *again*)

GLADYS. And what about that light in the bathroom?

FRED (*turning back to her*) We don't need a light in the bathroom if you'll leave the door open—there's enough light off the landing.

GLADYS. And do you expect Emma, Cissie and me to go in there and undress with the door open?

FRED. If you're all in together—you won't be able to shut it!

GLADYS (*turning away slightly down* L) It's the same with everything. Promises—promises—promises! The only thing you care for is pigeons—and what can they do?

FRED. Scratch behind their ears!

GLADYS. So can I!

FRED. With your toe?

GLADYS (*turning back*) No. But I can cook a dinner—wash clothes—and scrub floors. What have you got to say to that?

FRED. Have you tried sitting a couple of eggs?

GLADYS. All right. (*She sits on the downstage end of the settee*) But I'll tell you this. There's one pigeon coming home to roost that won't please you.

FRED. What's that?

GLADYS. The bill for this decorating.

FRED (*moving down* R) Don't forget you brought 'em in—not me! (*Turning on her*) And who's doing it?

GLADYS. A competent chap. Not an amateur like you.

FRED (*turning away again*) That rules out Charlie Gibbs, thank goodness! If I thought you'd got *that* old slap-dasher—(*as the thought strikes him, he stops suddenly, turns, moves* C *to the front of the table pointing his finger at Gladys*)—hey!

GLADYS. Well?

FRED. It isn't—is it?

GLADYS. Isn't what?

FRED. Charlie Gibbs?

GLADYS (*evasively*) D-d'you think I'd bring Charlie Gibbs in— knowing how you feel about him?

FRED (*turning away again*) No—I reckon you've more sense than that. All right. What's his name?

GLADYS. Whose name?

FRED (*turning to her; irately*) The decorator's!

GLADYS. Now let me see—was it . . .

(JOE DERBYSHIRE *appears at the top of the stairs*)

FRED (*almost shouting, and banging the bicycle saddle with his hand*) Answer me! I demand to know who did it!

JOE. I did.

FRED (*looking round*) *You* did? When?

JOE (*moving down to* R *of Fred*) Before you went to work this morning.

(EMMA *comes downstairs behind Joe and scuttles off through the door* R *into the kitchen*)

FRED (*incredulously*) *You* did this decorating?

JOE (*producing a bicycle pump from behind his back*) No—I borrowed your pump. I meant to tell you—but I forgot. I'm sorry, Fred.

(*The piston of the pump is fully extended*)

FRED. What did you want a pump for?

JOE (*producing a pipe in the other hand*) My pipe. It was blocked up. (*Holding it out almost under Fred's nose*)

(FRED *thrusts it away hurriedly*)

I couldn't blow through it, you see—so I put this end—(*indicating the lower end*)—into there—(*indicating the pipe bowl*)—and sucked up. And now they're both blocked up.

FRED. The pump as well?

JOE. I'm afraid so, it won't push down, you see. I reckon it's got a bit of dottle in its throttle.

FRED. Well, of all the daft tricks! How can I manage with it like that?

JOE. Don't upset yourself now. I've thought of a way.

FRED. What's that?

JOE (*producing string from his pocket*) I'll tie it under the cross-bar.

FRED (*snatching the pump*) Here—give it to me! (*After a struggle he forces it down*) Now—stick it back in its place!

(JOE *takes the pump and restores it to its position on the bicycle*)

Did the pigeon get back?

JOE. Oh yes—she was here long before dark.

FRED. That's good. We must keep her tuned up for the big race. Well—shove the bike out and lock up the pigeon shed. Come on—get a move on!

JOE. Right, Fred.

(JOE *picks up the bike bodily to turn it round. He hits Fred in the process.* FRED *opens the door* L *while* JOE *wheels it out*)

GLADYS. The way you order him about—anybody would think he was a servant.

FRED (*coming behind the settee*) And the way you women butter him up—anybody would think he was a slice o' bread!

GLADYS (*rising*) Anyway, I must be off to mother's. (*She crosses to the door* R, *behind the table where she stops to pick up the tea-tray*) I'll get your tea and Joe's supper. (*Stopping at the door* R) By the way—could you eat a bit of roast pork?

FRED. Not half!

GLADYS. That's good. I've ordered some for Sunday!

(GLADYS *exits to the kitchen* R)

FRED. Well, of all the . . . ! (*Going up* C)

(JOE *enters through the door* L)

JOE. Fred! Have you noticed?

FRED. Noticed what?

JOE. Somebody's been decorating.

FRED. Now don't you start! (*He moves down* R) Tell me—how's Sky looking?

JOE (*by the window*) A bit black. I fancy it'll rain before morning.

FRED. Not that Sky—you fool! I mean *our* "Sky"—Furnival Skyranger! You know, Joe—she'll win that Cross-Channel Race as sure as eggs are eggs.

JOE. I'm not happy about it. (*He moves down* L *behind the settee*)

FRED. You mean the race?

JOE. No—the eggs. I know nothing about pigeons, mind you—but I've never liked the idea of taking those two eggs off her. After all—*she* laid 'em. (*He moves to the downstage end of the settee*)

FRED. But she can't sit them *and* keep in training. And your cousin at *The Bull and Butcher* found us a foster-mother. What's wrong with that?

Joe. It's not the same. (*He sits on the settee*) Those eggs are missing something.

Fred. What?

Joe. A mother's love!

Fred (*moving slightly towards Joe*) Don't be soft! They're not hatched yet. And when they are—well—we'll have two more champions. Just think of that?

Joe (*sadly*) Poor little things.

Fred. What do you mean—"poor little things"?

Joe. Well, how would you like to open your eyes on the world for the first time, and find yourself in bed with your stepmother?

Fred. Oh, be quiet! (*He moves to the armchair* R) Let's see—how long is it now before they'll hatch out?

Joe. Five days according to you.

Fred. What do you mean "according to me"?

Joe. Well, you're the midwife.

Fred. I'll be the undertaker as well in a minute! Come on—get your hat.

Joe. What for?

Fred. We're going round to *The Bull* to have a look at 'em.

(Joe *collects his bowler hat from the sideboard.*
     Cissie *enters* L *followed by* Peter)

Cissie. Hello, Dad—Uncle Joe! Are we interrupting? (*She comes* C *in front of the table*)

(Joe *sits again on the settee*)

Fred (*moving to the fireplace*) No. We're just going out.

Cissie (*to Peter*) Coming in for a minute?

Peter. Well, I—er—thanks very much. (*He moves* L *of the table*) How do you do, Mr Furnival. I've—I've brought her home.

Fred (*to Joe, ignoring Peter*) Are you ready?

Joe. Yes. (*He rises, holding his bowler*)

Peter (*moving across up* R *behind the table*) I said: "I've brought her home"—Mr Furnival?

Fred (*still ignoring him*) Now where did I put that pigeon-basket? (*He looks around the fireplace and in front of the armchair*)

Cissie (*in front of the table*) Dad! Peter's speaking to you!

Fred (*turning to her*) What's that?

Peter. I said—"I've brought her home".

Fred (*turning to him*) Well—what do you want—a receipt? (*Turning to Joe*) Joe! You've locked up the pigeon-shed?

Joe (*in front of the settee*) No.

Fred. But I told you to!

Joe. I didn't think I ought—with Sky still out.

Fred. Still out! You said she'd come home long ago!

B

JOE. So she did. But she wouldn't go in.

FRED. Where is she then?

JOE. Sitting on top of the shed with that seagull.

FRED (*angrily*) That seagull again! I'll give it seagull!

(FRED *rushes out through the door* L. JOE *makes to follow, then changes his mind as he spots the pigeon-basket over behind the armchair* R. *He crosses and picks it up*)

JOE (*sitting on the arm of the chair*) You know, Cissie—your father's a bit like a pigeon himself.

CISSIE. In what way?

JOE. Well—if there's something he doesn't want to see, he tucks his head under his wing.

PETER. Meaning he doesn't want to see me?

JOE. I don't think he minds *seeing* you—it's who he sees you *with*.

CISSIE. It's ridiculous. What has he got against Peter?

JOE. Only one thing. The stork dropped him down the wrong chimney.

PETER. I know what you mean—but I can't help my father—can I?

JOE. No—and your father doesn't help you! (*He rises*) Anyway . . . look out—I think he's coming back.

(FRED *enters* L *carrying a live pigeon*)

FRED (*to the pigeon*) Did naughtie birdie frighten poor little Sky? Did he? Ah! naughty birdie!

JOE. Is she all right?

FRED (*sitting on the downstage end of the settee*) D'you hear that, Sky? They leave you out to catch your death of cold—and then they ask if you're all right! I don't suppose they tell you when they're going to do some decorating—do they? No, they don't—do they not! And do they sniff at you when you've been eating peppermints? They do? I'm not surprised! But you don't need a hint about making your way home when you're not wanted. (*Looking towards Peter*) Not like some folk we could talk about if we wanted to—couldn't we? (*Suddenly becoming serious, looking at the pigeon*) Hello—what's the matter now?

JOE. Is something wrong? (*He moves down* L *to the* R *of Fred, carrying the pigeon-basket and bowler*)

FRED. I do believe she's got a touch of croup.

(CISSIE *and* PETER *move down* R)

JOE (*dubiously*) Is it the same as measles? (*Sitting beside Fred*)

FRED (*scornfully*) It's as much like measles as a gum-boil's like an ingrowing toe-nail!

JOE. But they're both painful.

FRED. So is doing the splits if you're a mermaid! Now—shall

we talk some sense. I'm taking this bird with us to *The Bull* to let your cousin see her. Give me the basket!

JOE. Which basket?

FRED. The pigeon basket. You're holding it!

JOE. Am I? (*He lifts it up from the floor*) Eh, so I am!

(JOE *opens the end of the pigeon-basket*, FRED *pops the pigeon in head first and* JOE *shuts it in*)

JOE. That's dangerous, you know!

FRED. What is?

JOE. That door.

FRED. How?

JOE. Well—if she popped her head back sharp—couldn't you chop it off?

FRED. You could—if her head was on the same end as her parson's nose! Now come on quickly—before they find out we're gone.

(FRED *pushes Joe in front of him.*
    JOE *exits* L *while* FRED *collects his cap from the table*)

CISSIE. What shall I tell Mum?

FRED (*turning*) Tell her if we're not back soon—to put the cat out—(*he moves to the door* L)—and—(*looking hard at Peter*)—anything else that doesn't live here!

(FRED *exits* L)

CISSIE (*by the fireplace*) Don't take any notice of him, Peter. Come over here and tell me about . . .

(GLADYS *enters from the kitchen* R *carrying a tray with their meal*)

GLADYS. Well—here it is at last. If you don't provide me with shillings for the meter you can't expect—(*behind the table, looking around*)—hello—where are they?

CISSIE. Gone out.

GLADYS. Where?

CISSIE. *The Bull*. They've taken Sky. Dad thinks it's got croup.

GLADYS (*resting the tray on the table*) Oh, he does—does he?

CISSIE. Mum! What do they give a pigeon for croup?

GLADYS. Judging by the smell of your father—bottled stout and potato crisps! I thought you two were going to the pictures?

PETER. We couldn't get in.

GLADYS. What about the fire-escape?

CISSIE. It was up with the chain.

GLADYS. And your pal—the operator?

PETER. Down with the 'flu.

GLADYS. Well, I can't stand here entertaining you. If you want something to pass the time, Cissie—show him the family album.

CISSIE. Oh, no!

GLADYS. Why not? I'm sure he'd like to see your father lying on a cushion sucking his big toe?

PETER. I would indeed! Is it a studio portrait?

GLADYS (*picking up the tray*) No—it's a snap with a box camera. I took it myself.

PETER (*astonished*) *You* took it! How old was he?

GLADYS. Twenty-seven. He'd just dropped a hammer on his foot!

(GLADYS *stalks off with the tray through the door* R *to the kitchen*)

CISSIE (*crossing below the downstage end of the settee to the sideboard*) Well? Do you want to see the skeletons in the family cupboard?

PETER. Not really. I was only trying to please your mother.

CISSIE. That's easy! Dad's the trouble.

PETER. He's a menace! He'll never give his consent to you and me getting married.

CISSIE (*coming in front of the settee*) You're frightened to death of him, aren't you?

PETER (*moving* L *towards Cissie*) That's not fair, Cissie. You know I love you. I'd do anything for you.

CISSIE. All right then. We'll run away. Everybody's doing it nowadays.

PETER. Where to?

CISSIE. Gretna Green.

PETER. Wait a minute—that's different! (*He half turns up* R)

CISSIE. Are you trying to back out?

PETER. No—but I don't think my mum would like it.

CISSIE. Why not?

PETER. She's promised me a "white wedding".

CISSIE. Really! Has she decided what flowers you'll carry?

PETER. Besides I've asked Bill Harris to be best man. So he'd have to elope with us as well.

CISSIE. I see. Well—if you won't elope—I'll find someone who *will!* (*Turning up* C)

PETER. But, Cissie—you can't do it all in a minute.

CISSIE. All right. We'll start making arrangements now. Come on—let's go. (*She moves towards the door* L)

PETER. Where?

CISSIE. To the milk bar.

PETER (*turning away* R) Cissie! This Gretna Green—it is in Scotland, isn't it?

CISSIE. Yes.

PETER (*turning to her*) Would I have to wear a kilt?

CISSIE (*up* L) Oh, come on!

(PETER *moves up* L *to join her*)

Sh! (*Pausing to listen*) No—the other way! (*Indicating the door* R)

PETER. What for?

CISSIE. Dad and Uncle Joe—they're back! Come along—quickly!

(CISSIE *and* PETER *cross and exit* R.
     FRED *and* JOE *enter* L)

FRED (*depositing the pigeon-basket on the sideboard, and coming down* L) Well—she hasn't got croup, thank goodness! That reminds me—while I was locking up the pigeon shed—what were you doing with my bike?

JOE (*who has deposited his bowler on the sideboard; sitting* L *of the table*) Putting it out at the front.

FRED. What for?

JOE. I thought you wouldn't mind if I went to work on it. By the way have you noticed—you've gone flat at the back?

FRED. I've *what!* (*Looking around behind himself*)

JOE. Not *you*, Fred—the *bike!* The back tyre. I've a shrewd suspicion it's punctured!

FRED. Listen, Sherlock . . . !

(GLADYS *enters* R. *She is dressed in a hat and coat and is pulling on her gloves*)

GLADYS (*at the door*) So you have condescended to come home! I suppose you'll be ready for something to eat?

FRED. Not half! What have we got?

GLADYS. Beans on toast.

FRED (*behind the settee*) *Ugh!* Bullets on leather!

GLADYS (*turning and calling through the door* R) Emma!

EMMA (*off* R) Yes?

GLADYS. Bring those plates. (*She moves* R *of the table, behind it*)

FRED (*crossing to the chair* R *of the table, removing his jacket, hanging it on the back of the chair, and sitting*) Beans on toast! Where's that bit o' cold meat? I rather fancied that!

GLADYS. So did the cat! (*Moving to the* L *end of the table*)

(EMMA *enters* R *with a tray, plates, tablecloth, cutlery, cups, teapot, salt, evening paper, etc.*)

EMMA. I'm afraid they're well done! (*Going to the back of the table, she begins to set it*)

(JOE *helps to spread the cloth*)

GLADYS (*up* L *of Joe*) Well, I'm leaving you to it. Mother'll be wondering where I've got to. (*To Fred*) Now don't forget. Chop some wood—bank the fire—lock the shed—milk bottles out—washing in—and don't leave any lights on! Is there anything else?

FRED. Yes. Can I sweep the chimney?

GLADYS. I've no time to listen to your nonsense. Good night, Emma! Good night, Joe! And as for you, Fred Furnival—have you no message for your poor mother-in-law? Not one little word?

FRED. Yes.

GLADYS. What is it?

FRED. Antidisestablishmentarianism! And if she'd like another —Llan-fair—whatever it is—gogogogoch!

GLADYS (*disgustedly*) Oh!

(*She flounces out, slamming the door* L)

FRED. Pass the salt, Joe. Emma! Where's the evening paper?

EMMA. Right there by your elbow.

(JOE *hands* FRED *the salt.* FRED *begins to pour it on to his beans on toast, and continues to do so all the while he is reading the headlines*)

FRED. Well, I must say these headlines look well side by side! "BISHOP CONDEMNS PLUNGING NECKLINES", "HAVE RUSSIANS SOMETHING BIGGER UP THEIR SLEEVES"? I should think that's doubtful myself, wouldn't you, Joe? (*He puts the paper down, picks up his knife and fork and takes a mouthful of baked beans. He splutters and grimaces, dropping the knife and fork*) Ugh! Pour us some tea, Emma!

(EMMA *pours the tea.* FRED *gazes fascinated at the watery stream emerging from the spout*)

Is that tea?

EMMA. It should be good. It's one and ninepence a packet.

FRED. Do they give coupons?

EMMA. Yes.

FRED. Well, next time brew the coupons!

(EMMA *comes down* L *from behind the table and goes to the sideboard for her knitting*)

JOE. When will the decorating be finished?

FRED. If anybody mentions that again—(*he picks up an extra piece of toast from his plate*)—I'll bludgeon 'em to death with this toast!

(*A loud knocking is heard at the front door* L.
JOE *rises and steps out* L)

(*To Emma*) And that reminds me—that son of Charlie Gibbs —he's started calling around again. Who's encouraging him? *You*—Emma?

EMMA. Certainly not. (*She crosses to the armchair* R *and sits*)

FRED. If I had my way that lad would never get across this doorstep.

EMMA. It's no use going on like that—just because you and his father don't see eye to eye.

FRED. As for his father—if he ever sets foot in here—I'll throw him out!

(JOE *reappears at the door* L)

JOE. What was that?

FRED. I said: "If Charlie Gibbs ever sets foot in here—I'll throw him out!"

JOE. Then I'd better rub you down. He's at the front door now.

FRED. Send him in.

JOE. He says he won't come in if you're here. He just wants a word with Gladys.

FRED (*rising*) Oh, he does—does he? (*He moves* C *in front of the table*) All right. Tell him I'm not here!

JOE. But you are . . . ?

FRED. Go on—tell him!

(JOE *exits* L.
*A moment later* CHARLIE *enters* L *followed by* JOE)

CHARLIE (*at the top end of the settee*) I'm sorry to bother you—but—(*he suddenly sees Fred*) Fred! Oh, well—it was Gladys I wanted. I'll call again. (*He turns to go out*)

(JOE *bars his way*)

FRED. Oh, no, you don't! Out with it! What have you come for?

CHARLIE. If you must know—my pipe.

FRED. Your *pipe!* What's *your* pipe doing here?

CHARLIE. I left it.

FRED. When?

CHARLIE. This afternoon. (*He goes over to the sideboard*) This is it. (*Picking up his pipe*)

(FRED *moves towards Charlie*)

FRED (*realization suddenly dawning*) Here—wait a minute! (*Turning to Emma*) Emma! This decorating—who's doing it? *Him?* (*Indicating Charlie*)

(EMMA *nods.* JOE *moves down behind the settee*)

FRED. So that's it! A conspiracy! (*He moves down* R) And you're all in it—all of you! All nice and secret, wasn't it?

CHARLIE. Secret? (*He goes to the step-ladders leaning against the back wall and turns them round. Lifting them up, he lets the audience see, neatly printed down the side in large white letters:* "C. GIBBS, DECORATOR".) Look there! Is there anything secret about that? (*Restoring the ladders to their former place*)

FRED (*moving* R *of the table*) I'll sue you! I'll summon you for unlawful entry! I can prove it wasn't done under my instructions!

CHARLIE (*coming down* L *of the table*) *Your* instructions! I wouldn't lift a finger to help you! I'm doing this for Gladys!

FRED (*returning* RC) I've a good mind to throw you out!

CHARLIE (LC) That'll be interesting. I remember seeing you toss a pigeon. (*Sneering*) And your Furnival Skyranger! You think it's a wonder, don't you? But there's something at our house that can lick it easily—my Smokey!

FRED. Smokey! What's that—a tomcat?

CHARLIE. It's a pigeon. And Smokey's going to show your bird how to fly the Channel.

FRED. Listen! When they're all clocked in—and the prize list published—do you know where my Sky'll be?

CHARLIE. Where?

FRED (*singing*) *On top of old Smokey.*

CHARLIE. We'll see. (*He moves up* L) Anyway, I'm walking out on this job!

FRED. Good!

CHARLIE. I'll be in the morning to collect my stuff.

FRED. You won't need. It'll be outside on the pavement.

(EMMA *moves behind the table and begins clearing the pots on to the tray*)

CHARLIE (*at the* L *end of the table; angrily*) This is my last word to you, Fred Furnival. You're a conceited, pig-headed, big-mouthed, old wind-bag! Good night! (*Moving to the door* L)

FRED. And the same to you with zip-fasteners!

CHARLIE (*at the door* L) Bah!

(CHARLIE *slams the door behind him as he exits.*
JOE *sits on the downstage end of the settee.* FRED *moves* RC)

EMMA (*behind the table*) If you've finished the fun and games—isn't it about time you thought of going to work, Joe Derbyshire?

JOE. Oh heck! I'm forgetting. (*He rises*) Where's my flask and sandwiches?

EMMA (*picking up the tray*) I'll go and get them.

(*She exits to the kitchen* R. *There is a slight pause after her exit, during which* JOE *sits again on the settee and produces a pipe and matches*)

FRED. You're looking a bit off, Joe! (*Moving behind the settee to the sideboard cupboard*) You need a drop of something.

JOE. No—I daresn't! Somebody might smell me.

FRED (*behind the settee down* L) Not if you light that pipe—they won't get near enough! (*Producing a bottle from the cupboard, and holding it over the back of the settee in front of Joe's face*) There! Look at that.

JOE. What is it?

FRED (*turning back to the sideboard and producing two glasses. He uncorks the bottle and proceeds to pour half a tumbler for Joe, and a full one for himself*) A souvenir from the war. "*Arrack*" the natives call it—otherwise known as "*Still Dynamite*". The last time I had a do on it was Christmas Day, 1944. What a day!

JOE. You'll never forget it?

FRED. I'll never remember it! There you are—(*he hands a half-filled tumbler to* JOE)—Try that! (*He crosses below the settee to* RC *carrying a full tumbler and the Arrack bottle*)

JOE. I shouldn't, really. (*Rising to toast Fred*) Ah well—skin off your nose!

FRED (*returning the toast*) Lining off your stomach!

(*As they drink there is a knock at the door* L)

FRED. If that's Charlie Gibbs looking for his tobacco pouch— I'll brain him!

(FRED *crosses to the door* L *placing his glass on the* L *end of the table in passing. At the door he stands with his back to the audience brandishing the bottle.* JOE *sits again on the downstage end of the settee. The knocking is repeated at the door* L)

Come in!

(FRED *raises the bottle in his hand as the door* L *slowly opens, he is about to strike when the door is suddenly pushed wide.*
JIM DOBSON, *the policeman, is revealed. He is in uniform*)

JIM. Hallo—hallo! What's going on?

FRED (*quickly holding up the bottle and pretending to look at it against the light*) Nothing, Jim. I just thought this stuff was corked.

JIM (*moving down* C) I hope you don't mind my coming straight in—the outside door was open.

FRED (*turning to him; jokingly*) Have you got a warrant?

JIM. Well—no. (*He moves down* R) Though I s'pose I could call it an official visit if I wanted to.

FRED (*moving* C) All right. I can take a hint. What's up?

JIM (*pointing in the direction of the door* L) Outside your front gate—on the public highway—there's a bicycle parked!—without lights!

FRED. Well, what do you want me to do? Turn it upside down and stand there turning the pedals?

JIM. You could *shift* it!

JOE. I'll move it, Jim. (*Rising and going* L *of the settee towards the door* L) It was me that put it there.

JIM (*pointing at him and stopping him by the upstage end of the settee*) Wait a minute! (*Unbuttoning the top pocket of his tunic*) You realize I'm only doing my duty? (*Producing a notebook*)

FRED. Do you mean you're going to book him?

JIM. No, no! But there is something you might be interested in. We're holding a draw down at *The Red Lion*—the Darts Club— (*taking tickets from the notebook*)—tickets—threepence each—or a book of eleven for half a crown. First prize—value twenty pounds. Shall we say—two books apiece?

FRED (*quietly*) I see. (*To Joe*) Joe! Give him a ten-bob note.

JOE (*finding a note*) What for?

FRED. We've been fined—five bob apiece!

(FRED *takes the note, hands it to* JIM, *who in turn hands the tickets to Fred, and* JIM *puts the ten shilling note in his trouser pocket*)

JIM (*restoring his notebook and buttoning his top pocket*) Thanks very much—you're very generous! (*Staring hard at the bottle in Fred's hand*) Thirsty weather—isn't it?

FRED (*to Joe*) All right. Bring another glass.

JOE. What for?

FRED. It's five bob—*and* costs!

(JOE *goes over to the sideboard to fetch a glass*)

JIM (*raising a protesting hand*) I'm on duty—you know! (*He lowers his hand*) Still I think it'll be all right if I remove this. (*He takes off his helmet and puts it down on the* R *end of the table*) After all— I can't have it in my helmet, can I?

FRED (*taking a glass from Joe*) You can't! You'll have it in a glass like everybody else.

(JIM *sits in the armchair* R. FRED *pours at the table a third of a glass and hands it to* JIM. *He also refills his own glass*)

JIM. Well—good health all! (*He takes a drink, rolls it round his tongue, and swallows*) Hm! Aniseed cordial! (*He drains the glass and pointedly up-ends it*) It's more-ish, isn't it?

FRED (*snatching up the bottle from the table and handing it to Joe*) No —it's Algerian!

(JOE *puts the bottle back in the sideboard cupboard*)

JIM. By the way—how's the bird?

FRED (*draining his glass and setting it down on the table*) Sky? She's fine!

JIM. She'll win?

FRED. Nothing surer?

JIM (*rising*) In that case—(*he sets his glass down on the table, picks up his helmet and dons it, puts his hand in his trouser pocket and produces a ten shilling note and handing it to Fred*)—here's your ten bob back!

FRED. What for?

JIM. Get it on with Big Sam, the bookie. (*He crosses in front of Fred up* L)

FRED. Couldn't you get it on yourself?

JIM (*turning*) It wouldn't seem proper.

FRED. Why? Aren't you speaking?

JIM. As a matter of fact—he's just bought eight books of draw tickets.

FRED. Well, he won't hold that against you?

JIM. He will. You see he's still getting that summons for speeding! (*moving to the door* L) Ah well—just behave yourselves. And remember—don't do anything I wouldn't! So long!

(JIM *exits* L)

JOE. Well—of all the cool customers! (*The door* R *opens*) He just about takes the biscuit!

(EMMA *enters* R *from the kitchen carrying a flask, a parcel of sandwiches and a wicker basket full of empty milk bottles. As she enters* FRED *snatches the two glasses from the table and passes them to* JOE *who stows them in the sideboard cupboard*)

EMMA. No, you're not taking any biscuits! There's your flask and sandwiches. Now off you go!

JOE. There's no hurry! I've got Fred's bicycle.

FRED. *And* Fred—to keep you company!

EMMA (*behind the table; setting down her basket*) To keep him company?

FRED (*crossing to the chair* R *of the table and collecting his jacket*) I'm going with him!

EMMA. What for?

FRED (*donning his jacket*) I feel like a walk.

JOE. But what about the bike?

FRED (*collecting the flask and sandwiches from the table*) That's all right. *You* ride there—*I* ride back! (*Crossing to Joe by the sideboard and handing him the flask and sandwiches*)

JOE. But if I'm riding—and you're walking . . . ?

FRED (*picking up Joe's bowler from the sideboard and planting it on Joe's head*) If you'll stop nattering—we'll have time for a call at *The Bull* as well. (*He collects his own cap*)

JOE. What for?

FRED (*winking and digging Joe in the ribs*) To see those eggs. Come on! (*He moves up to the door* L) 'Night, Emma. And don't wait up. I've got my key!

(FRED *disappears through the door* L *leaving it open*)

JOE (*following him up* L, *turning to Emma just in front of the open door*) Good night, love.

EMMA (*coolly*) Good night.

JOE. Aren't you going to kiss me?

(FRED *reappears* L)

FRED. Not in front of Emma! Come on!

(FRED *grabs* JOE *and fairly snatches him off through the door* L. *As they go* FRED'S *voice breaks into song and then dies away.*

EMMA, *picking up the basket of milk bottles, also goes out* L. *She can be heard calling the cat*)

EMMA (*off*) Puss, puss, puss! Oh well—stop out then! (*She raises her voice*) And keep away from that rhubarb—you nasty thing!

EMMA *re-enters* L, *closing the door behind her. She carries the empty wicker basket which she puts on the sideboard, she picks up a torch, glances all round her and then switches off the light by the door* L. EMMA *exits upstairs* R *shining her torch as*—

*the* CURTAIN *falls*

*When the* CURTAIN *rises after a brief interval, to denote the passage of time, a rattling can be heard at the front door* L.

CISSIE (*off*) It's a good job I'd got my key.
PETER (*off*) Have they gone out?
CISSIE (*off*) They've gone to bed! Didn't you notice the milk bottles?

(CISSIE *enters* L *and switches on the light*)

CISSIE. Well? (*She moves* C) Aren't you coming in?

(PETER *enters* L)

PETER (*closing the door*) Do you think I ought?
CISSIE. Why not?
PETER. With them being in bed—it doesn't seem proper.
CISSIE (*moving down* R) You do need jolting out of yourself—don't you? You're about as romantic as a cold rice pudding. (*Archly*) Peter?
PETER. Yes?
CISSIE. Come here!
PETER (*moving towards her, down* R) Now what's up?
CISSIE (*putting her hands behind her back*) Kiss me!
PETER. What?
CISSIE (*tilting her head back, pouting her lips by way of invitation, and closing her eyes*) I said: kiss me!
PETER (*glancing nervously round*) N-now?
CISSIE (*firmly*) Now!
PETER. W-with the light on?
CISSIE (*equally firmly*) With the light on!

(PETER *leans forward and essays a very perturbed peck. Finding he likes it, he lingers on it, and gradually his arms steal around her and they become locked in a loving embrace*)

CISSIE (*breathlessly, leaning back*)  There! How did you like that?
PETER. *Smashing!*
CISSIE.  So we're going to elope?
PETER.  Yes—but . . . !
CISSIE.  The only thing we haven't settled is—*when.*
PETER.  Never mind. We can talk about it again. (*Making to kiss her again*)
CISSIE (*pushing him away*)  Oh, no! There won't be time.
PETER.  Why not?
CISSIE.  Because we're going to elope *now—tonight!*
PETER.  Tonight? We can't!
CISSIE.  And why can't we?
PETER.  Because—well—if you must know—I don't know how to!
CISSIE (*astonished*)  You don't know how to?
PETER.  That's why we can't do it tonight. We've got to have a practice first.
CISSIE.  What a wonderful idea! A rehearsal—a trial elopement! Peter—you're a genius!
PETER (*modestly*)  I wouldn't say that.
CISSIE.  Now—how would you begin?
PETER.  Well—when they're all in bed—you slip down—I meet you at the front door—and off we go!
CISSIE.  There you are, see! You haven't a clue! *I* shall make *my* exit through the bedroom window. And *you've* got to provide a ladder!
PETER (*going back up* R *to the painter's ladders*)  What about this? Will it reach?
CISSIE.  Take it outside and try it.
PETER.  O.K.! (*He picks up the ladders and crosses to the door* L)
CISSIE.  Wait a minute! Where are you going?
PETER (*turning and smiling tolerantly*)  To put the ladder by the window.
CISSIE.  Which?
PETER (*still smiling*)  Yours.
CISSIE.  And you know which it is?
PETER.  Er—(*smile dissolves*)—no!
CISSIE (*at the end* R *of the table*)  You see? The first thing you know you'll be rushing up that ladder and finding Auntie Emma waiting for you! Can you imagine anything worse?
PETER.  Yes—finding your father!
CISSIE.  My bedroom is directly over this window. (*Pointing to the box-window*)  Now—put the ladder by the side of it—quickly and quietly!

(PETER, *carrying the ladders, exits* L. CISSIE *then alternates between the foot of the stairs and the* R *end of the box-window, listening anxiously and looking out* L.
    PETER *re-enters* L)

PETER. Right! The next thing?

CISSIE (*coming down behind the armchair*) You've got to go home!

PETER. Go home? (*Moving to the upstage end of the settee*) But I thought we were . . . ?

CISSIE. So we are. (*Down* R) You won't go with just the things you stand up in—will you? Now you go off home and pack a bag as quickly as you can!

PETER. All right. When I come back—what do I do?

CISSIE. Climb the ladder and tap on the window. Got it?

PETER. Yes. (*Moving down* C) Before I go—Cissie!

CISSIE. Yes?

PETER. Come here!

CISSIE (*approaching*) What's the matter now?

PETER. *Kiss me!*

CISSIE. Oh, Peter! My caveman!

(*They embrace and kiss*)

PETER (*breaking it up and moving to the door* L) Before you know where you are—I'll be climbing that window and tapping on the ladder! *Yipee!*

> (PETER *rushes off through the door* L, *leaving it open.*
> CISSIE *follows him*)

CISSIE (*off*) I'll leave the front door unlocked so we can get back in afterwards.

> (CISSIE *enters* L *carrying a suitcase which she drops on the settee and opens. She then goes to a drawer in the sideboard and takes out some articles of clothing which she stuffs in the suitcase. As she moves to the sideboard for a second consignment* FRED *and* JOE *can be heard rendering* "Bless 'Em All". CISSIE *rushes to the window*)

CISSIE (*looking towards the* L *of the window*) Dad!

> (CISSIE *then rushes to the suitcase, shuts it, picks it up and going to the door* L *she switches off the light. She then scuttles upstairs* R.
> *The singing grows louder and suddenly there is a crash and a cry off* L, *milk bottles are heard rolling about*)

FRED (*off* L, *in a thick loud voice*) Who left that ladder there? Who lef' that ladder there! If it'sh the window-cleaner, I'll wring his wash-leather! (*He pauses*) Joe! Hold the door. Shomebody's waving it about! Wait a minute I've got a better idea. When the door comes pasht—you shove me—and I'll stab it! Right—*shove!*

> (*A dull thud is heard*)

Thatsh the idea! Now all we've got to do is find the key!

> (FRED *begins to sing again.*
> *The beam of a torch is seen to descend the stairs* R *and travel to the*

*door* L, *suddenly the light flashes on and* EMMA *is revealed, in her night-gown and curlers. She stands by the switch and listens nervously*)

Have you jusht struck a match? You haven't? You know what? Dawnsh breaking! Right—shove!

(*There is a loud clatter outside the door* L *and* EMMA *rushes up the stairs again and stands on the top step.*
FRED *enters* L)

Thash funny! I still haven't found the key. All right—bring that ladder in! Teach that window-cleaner a lesshon!

(*A very dazed* JOE *enters* L *carrying the painter's ladders, which he lays on the floor, horizontally in front of the trestle table.* FRED *closes the door and moves* C)

EMMA (*coming to the bottom step and folding her arms*) Well?
FRED. Oh—excuse me, lady—(*he raises his cap*)—can we—can we . . .
EMMA. Can you what?
FRED. Carol-shing?

(JOE *comes down* L *behind the settee with his bowler still on. He holds himself very carefully erect as though at any moment he might spill over. He stands in front of the settee swaying slightly back and forth, then he gradually subsides into the downstage end, his cheeks bulging now and then and with a dazed and glassy look in his eyes*)

EMMA (*moving* C) What's the meaning of this? (*To Joe*) Why aren't you at work?
FRED (*removing his cap and placing it on the table*) Because he's not going!
EMMA. Not going?
FRED. He's not going to that old warehoushe any more! He's stoppin' at home—aren't you, Joe? He's stoppin' at home—an' they're bringin' the warehoushe to him!
EMMA (*almost tearfully*) Drunk! My Joe—drunk!
FRED. How do you know? Are you a qualified medical pra—pra—(*Starting again*) Are you a qualified medical practish-tish-tish . . .
JOE (*subconsciously*) Bless you!
FRED (*to Joe*) Shut up! (*To Emma again*) Are you a—doctor? Well *are* you? You shee—you don't know! Itsh *you* that's drunk—both of you! (*Pointing a finger at Emma and an imaginary figure beside her*)
EMMA (*moving up* R) I'm going to bed!
FRED. Oh, no—you're not! Sit down!
EMMA. Certainly not!
FRED (*raising his voice aggressively*) I said: "Sit down!" (*Shouting*) Go on! Sit down!

(EMMA *sits rather fearfully in the armchair* R)

(*Going to Joe; proudly*) Thash the way they handle police-dogs! (*He sits* R *of Joe*) Now—we'll get on with the performansh!

(FRED *claps his hands slowly twice and stares at Emma.* EMMA *sits nervously twisting her handkerchief.* FRED *claps again*)

(*Beckoning to Emma*) Hey! Fatima! Come here!

(EMMA *is reluctant*)

(*Shouting*) Come here!

(EMMA *rises and scuttles over to him like a frightened rabbit*)

You know what that meansh? (*He claps again*) It means: "Bring on the dancing girls!"

EMMA. B-but there are no dancing girls!

FRED (*to Joe*) D'you hear that? No dancing girls!

JOE. Pity! (*Ever since sitting down Joe's eyes have been fixed in a glassy stare straight out in front of him. He never looks at either Fred or Emma*)

FRED (*to Emma*) Never mind—you'll do, Fatima! Where's your seven veils?

EMMA (*horrified*) Seven veils?

FRED (*rising*) I'll get 'em for you.

(FRED *goes to the pasting-board under the window and picks up half a dozen cut lengths of wallpaper which have been specially prepared. He brings them down to Emma and slaps them down on her head so that it goes through the cuts which have been prepared in the centre of them all. They hang down on her back and front, one on top of another.*

*During this episode* PETER *appears outside the box-window looking for his ladders. Spotting them inside he disappears*)

(*Returning to sit beside Joe*) Right—off we go! Play the music! (*He begins to groan out an Indian snake-charmer's tune*) Come on—woman—dance!

(*To placate him,* EMMA *breaks into a very dignified polka*)

(*Stopping his singing*) No—no—no! That won't do. (*Rising*) Use your arms like this, (*he strikes an Egyptian pose*) and walk up and down like this! (*He does a few steps across to* R *and back* L) Now—try again.

(FRED *flops down beside Joe, and resumes singing: "Da-da-dar-dar-dar! Da-da-da-da-da-da-da-dar!" He claps his hands to the beat, nudging Joe, until* JOE, *too, begins clapping mechanically, although still gazing before him with unseeing eyes*)

(*Interrupting his singing*) First veil! (*He sings again*)

(EMMA *rips off the top sheet of wallpaper and sheds it*)

(*As before*) Second veil!

> (EMMA *casts another sheet.*
> PETER *has crept in through the door* L. *He has just got his hands on the ladder, when* FRED *turns round sharply*)

(*Rising*) Shtop the music!
PETER. I-I'm sorry, Mr Furnival—I—it's the ladder. My father wants it back you see.
FRED (*up* C *beside Peter*) D'you hear that, Joe? The window-cleaner's boy! Come and sit down.
PETER. Really—I ...
FRED (*forcing him towards the settee*) Come and sit down! (FRED *forces* PETER *to sit between himself and Joe. He himself sits on the upstage arm of the settee*)
PETER. Well—thank you very much.
FRED. You're welcome! (*To Emma*) Right—action! (*He begins the singing and clapping again*)

> (JOE *claps like an automaton.* FRED *gestures to* PETER *to clap, until he, too, joins in*)

(*As before*) Third veil!

> (EMMA *sheds another*)

(*To Peter*) Come on—shing up!

> (PETER *joins in with the song too*)

(*To Peter*) The next one's yours. Shout up!

PETER. *Fourth veil!*

> (EMMA *sheds another.*
> CISSIE *appears at the top of the stairs. She stands staring in amazement*)

FRED. This is mine! *Number five!*

> (EMMA *sheds another*)

(*To Peter*) Passht to you!

PETER. *Sixth veil!*

> (EMMA *sheds the last piece of wallpaper, and stops dancing. She stands* C *sobbing into her handkerchief*)

FRED (*silencing his orchestra*) Now what's the trouble?
EMMA. It's finished! (*She is now* C, R *of Fred and near enough to him for him to touch her without moving*)
FRED. Finished? (*Grabbing her nightdress*) You've still got this one! *Come on—off with it!* (*He starts singing and clapping again*)

> (CISSIE *comes tearing downstairs and down* C)

C

CISSIE (*between Fred and Emma*) Stop it! Do you hear? *Stop it!*

(FRED *stops singing, he stares open-mouthed*)

How dare you behave like that! You drunken beasts—all of you!

(FRED *is still clapping foolishly, but his hands are missing one another*)

FRED. B-but itsh all good clean fun!

CISSIE (*turning from comforting Emma*) Good clean fun! To think my own father could behave like that! (*To Joe*) As for you, Uncle Joe—you're a monster! To stand by and see your own wife humiliated! What have *you* got to say for yourself?

JOE (*still staring forward*) Pity!

CISSIE (*to Peter*) And *you* . . . !

PETER. Look, Cissie—I can explain everything.

CISSIE. Well, if you're so good at explaining—here's one thing you can go on explaining for the rest of your life!

PETER. What's that?

CISSIE. I never want to see you again—ever! (*To Emma*) Come on, Auntie!

(CISSIE *leads the sobbing* EMMA *off up the stairs*)

PETER (*following them up* R *to the foot of the stairs*) But, Cissie . . . ?

CISSIE. Good-bye!

(EMMA *and* CISSIE *disappear*)

FRED (*shaking his head and turning to Joe*) Have I shaid anything wrong?

(JOE's *head is now sunk, he is asleep, his hands crossed on his chest.* FRED, *getting no response, turns to Peter, but* PETER *is still staring up the stairs*)

FRED (*to Peter*) Window-cleaner! Have I shaid anything wrong?

PETER (*moving* C *and turning on him*) I've only one thing to say to you.

FRED. Whash that?

PETER. You're an interfering, silly, intoxicated, old fool! Good night!

(PETER *slams out of the door* L)

FRED (*turning back to Joe*) Joe! (*He shakes him*) Joe! (*But Joe does not wake*) You're vexed with me—aren't you? (*He begins to sing* "Red Sails in the Sunset". *He rises and peels off his jacket as he goes towards the table. Stopping his song he turns to look at Joe and a smile flits across his face, then he sings again. He moves to the upstage end of the settee and picks up Charlie Gibbs' white painter's coat and puts it on, again stopping his song*) Ah well! Back to work! (*He sings again as he goes to the pasting-board and picks up a piece of wallpaper and the paste-*

*bucket. Returning to the settee he puts the bucket on the settee beside Joe, removing Joe's bowler hat. He then puts the wallpaper around Joe's neck like a barber's apron, and leans over the back of the settee to Joe)* Shampoo—sir? Shertainly!

FRED *scoops a double handful of paste out of the bucket and begins to work it vigorously but clumsily into Joe's hair with both hands, bellowing out "Red Sails in the Sunset" as—*

*the* CURTAIN *falls*

# ACT II

SCENE—*The same. Early the following morning.*

*When the* CURTAIN *rises the room resembles a nightmare scene. The* L *half of the set as decorated by Charlie Gibbs is still neat and tidy except for the door* L *which has been loosely papered over and hidden from view. The* R *half is criss-crossed with wallpaper in a crazy fashion. The box-window is partly obscured with loose hanging, twisted folds of paper; the stag's head over the fireplace is covered except for the horns which are sticking through two torn holes. Completely hidden under lengths of wall-paper,* FRED *lies on the settee. As he snores the paper rises and falls rhythmically. Wallpaper litters the floor.*

*EMMA enters* R *from the stairs. She studies the scene in wide-eyed amazement.*

EMMA. Mercy on us! Whatever's happened! (*She comes down to the back of the settee and puts a hand under the wallpaper shaking the sleeping Fred*) Joe!

(FRED *grunts*)

Joe, love! (*Irately*) Wake up—will you!

(FRED *turns uneasily, rises from a reclining to a sitting position and his tousled head emerges through the paper. He is still wearing his white painter's coat*)

Oh—it's you, is it? And what do you think's ailing you? (*She moves to the top of the settee*)

FRED. Sunstroke!

EMMA. Where is he?

FRED. Who?

EMMA. Joe!

FRED (*rummaging under the wallpaper*) I don't know. I'll have a look.

EMMA. You needn't bother. (*She moves* C) The bird's flown, I'll bet. And when he saw this lot—I don't blame him!

FRED. Saw what lot? (*Looking around the room*) Ugh! Emma! Whatever made you do it? Well, I'll bet you're relieved you've got that out of your system!

EMMA (*aghast*) You don't think *I* did it?

FRED. Well, if *you* didn't—who did? Joe?

EMMA. He might have helped!

FRED. Helped who?

EMMA. You!

FRED (*bewildered*) Me! You don't believe I . . . ?

Emma. After that seven veils—I can believe anything!

Fred. What seven veils?

Emma. So you don't remember anything about last night?

Fred (*holding his head*) Let me see? Yes. I took Sky to Joe's cousin—I had a row with Charlie Gibbs—Jim Dobson let me in for some draw tickets—then—well, I suppose Joe went to work, and I went to bed.

Emma. Joe *didn't* go to work—he was incapable! And your bed's not been slept in!

Fred (*astounded*) It hasn't? (*Sudden thought*) Emma! You don't think I got into the wrong . . . ?

Emma. *My* door was locked! Besides you've got a shocking head—you were asleep fully dressed under all this stuff—you've got paste all over you—and you smell like a brewer's yard! What does that sound like?

Fred (*realizing*) *Arrack! That's it—Arrack!*

Emma. I don't know what Gladys'll say!

Fred (*rising*) She mustn't know!

Emma. If Cissie doesn't tell her—I shall!

Fred. Was *Cissie* in this? (*He sits down again*)

Emma. But for her, I wouldn't be able to look you in the face.

Fred. We'll have to think of some way out. You leave it to me. Don't say a word!

Emma. Don't worry—I'm going to say plenty!

Fred (*menacingly*) *You're* not going to say a word!

Emma. When Gladys hears about your behaviour . . .

Fred (*quickly*) And Joe's! When she hears how he took me out and got me drunk—how he over-persuaded me, and I was weak . . .

Emma (*uncertainly*) Are you telling the truth?

Fred. You ask Joe!

Emma. The state he was in—I don't suppose he'll remember.

Fred (*aside*) I hope not! (*Quickly*) You say he didn't go to work?

Emma. No. He came back with you. You said he wasn't going any more.

Fred (*putting on an act*) Ah yes! I'm beginning to remember. I begged him—pleaded with him—but he just laughed in my face!

Emma. The monster!

(*There is a slight pause*)

Fred (*quietly and slyly*) Suppose they find out at the warehouse why he didn't turn up?

Emma. They couldn't possibly!

Fred (*menacing again*) You never know. If anyone were to tell Gladys—they might!

Emma. You mean you'd . . . ?

FRED. I'd do anything to keep it from Gladys! (*Sweetly*) I think we understand one another—eh—Emma?

EMMA. What about Cissie?

FRED. I can fix her!

EMMA (*pointing to the general confusion*) But can you fix this?

FRED. That's the problem! (*Holding his head*) If only my head would clear!

EMMA. Should I get you a glass of water?

FRED (*indignantly*) Look! If you found a chip-pan blazing on a gas-stove, would you stick it under the tap?

EMMA. Certainly not!

FRED. Then don't suggest putting water in this! (*Pointing to his stomach*)

EMMA. Well, I'm sure I don't know how you're going to explain. Gladys is bound to . . .

(*She is interrupted by a loud knocking at the front door*)

FRED. What's that? (*Holding his head and screwing up his eyes*)

EMMA. Somebody knocking.

FRED. Well, tell 'em to stop it. They're fracturing my skull!

(*The knocking is repeated*)

(*Rising, and approaching by instinct where the door* L *should be*) Who's there?

GLADYS (*off* L) It's me—Gladys! I can't find my key!

FRED (*up by the door* L) I can't find the door! (*He tears down one of the lengths of wallpaper over the door*)

GLADYS (*off*) Is anything wrong?

FRED. No, no! I-I'll let you in in a minute!

GLADYS (*off*) But I don't want to come in!

FRED (*hardly believing his ears*) You don't *want* to come in?

GLADYS (*off*) No. I've got to call at the surgery for mother's prescription. I'll be back as soon as I can. Bye-bye!

FRED. Bye-bye, love! Don't hurry! (*He comes down* C *wiping his forehead*)

(CISSIE *appears at the top of the stairs, carrying the clothes she removed from the sideboard drawer in Act I to put into the suitcase*)

(*To Emma*) That was a narrow squeak?

EMMA (*moving down* R) It's only prolonging the agony!

FRED. A good thing it happened, though. It's cleared my head! (*He starts removing the white painter's coat, and begins to put on his own jacket, which is still lying on the table*)

(CISSIE *crosses down* L *to the sideboard*)

(*Noticing Cissie for the first time*) Oh, good morning, Cissie love!

(CISSIE *ignores him. She starts putting clothes into the sideboard drawer*)

FRED. I—I wonder if you'd like to do something for me?

(CISSIE *with her back to him merely bangs the drawer*)

I'm talking to you—Cissie!

(CISSIE *still ignores him*)

Haven't you one word for your own father?

CISSIE (*turning*) Yes—beast!

FRED. All right—*Beauty!* But don't forget—you and your Prince Charming might want a bit of help one day! I'm in a tight corner, Cissie—you've got to help me!

CISSIE. How?

FRED. By keeping quiet.

CISSIE. You just wait till mum gets home!

FRED. I don't see why you need fuss. (*With a sly look at Emma*) Aunt Emma's on my side—aren't you, Emma?

CISSIE (*moving down* L *below the settee, with one article still in her hand, to Emma*) Do you mean *you*—aren't going to say anything?

EMMA. No. I-I'm prepared to let bygones be bygones!

FRED (*to Cissie*) You see! Now if you'll promise not to . . .

CISSIE (*firmly*) Not me! (*She turns back to the sideboard and places the last article in the drawer*)

FRED (*smoothly*) Well, I think we can come to a friendly agreement if we have a little chat afterwards. Shall we say you'll keep quiet for the present?

CISSIE (*turning to Fred*) Only if . . .

FRED. That's fine! You'll lend a hand with this mess? (*Indicating the crazy wallpapering*)

CISSIE (*looking around*) I suppose I'll have to—whether Mum knows or not.

FRED. All right—let's begin. (*To Cissie*) Go round to Charlie Gibbs and tell him to come here right away.

EMMA. Whatever for?

FRED (*to Emma*) Don't ask questions! (*To Cissie, shepherding her towards the door* L) Off you go—quick!

(*As* CISSIE *reaches the door* L *there is a loud knocking at the front door*)

(*To Cissie*) Wait! It might be your mother!

(*The knocking is repeated more urgently*)

(*At the door* L, *shouting*) Was the doctor busy, love?

CHARLIE (*off* L; *shouting*) He will be if somebody doesn't get my stuff out!

FRED (*to Emma and Cissie*) All right. Leave this to me!

(FRED *motions to Cissie and Emma to go.*
EMMA *goes off up the stairs.*
CISSIE *goes through the door* R. FRED *opens the door* L *and goes through into the hall*)

(*Off*) Charlie! You're just in time!
CHARLIE (*off*) I thought my stuff was going to be out on the pavement?

(FRED *re-enters* L)

FRED. I've changed my mind. I've been having a look at what you've done, you see—and . . .
CHARLIE (*off*) Well?
FRED (*coming down* C) I like it! Yes, I like it! So I've decided to let you finish the job.

(CHARLIE *enters* L)

CHARLIE (*sarcastically*) Oh, you have—have you? (*His eye suddenly takes in the scene. His jaw drops, his eyes protrude*)

(WILLIE *enters* L)

WILLIE (*up* L *just inside the room; excitedly*) What a smashing scheme. Did you get it out of the trade journal?
CHARLIE (*down* C, L *of Fred*) Have they recaptured him?
FRED. Who?
CHARLIE. The lunatic!
FRED (*swallowing hard*) Look, Charlie—it's nothing like that. (*Turning down* R) I just thought I'd try my hand.
CHARLIE (*incredulously*) *You* did this?
FRED (*turning back to him*) Well—I'm out of practice.
CHARLIE. You're out of your mind! (*Turning to Willie*) Hey—you! 'Op it!
WILLIE. Oh, don't be a spoil-sport!
CHARLIE. Go and mind the cart!
WILLIE (*annoyed*) O.K.! But I'll tell you one thing!
CHARLIE. What's that?
WILLIE. There are times when I hate you!

(WILLIE *sticks his tongue out at Charlie and exits hurriedly* L)

FRED (*moving down* R) Listen, Charlie—it's not easy to explain—but say you'd drained a bottle of whisky—couldn't *you* do something like this?
CHARLIE. I couldn't match it if I'd drained a distillery! So you were tight, eh? (*He laughs and sits on the settee*) What did Gladys say?
FRED. She doesn't know yet! And when she does—it's up to you.
CHARLIE. What d'you mean?

FRED. Well, you're doing the job—if you were to tell Gladys that you . . .

CHARLIE (*rising; angrily*)  Are you asking *me* to say that *I* did this?

FRED. Well—I—er . . .

CHARLIE. I wouldn't do it for my own brother! It'd ruin me!

FRED. I'm not asking you to take the rap. Only to help me?

CHARLIE (*scornfully*)  Help *you?* (*He laughs and sits down again*) For Pete's sake!

FRED. No—for Smokey's!

CHARLIE (*suspiciously*)  What d'you mean?

FRED. I'll tell you. In the big race—which bird is the greatest danger to your Smokey?

CHARLIE. You know damn well! Furnival Skyranger.

FRED (*moving down* C)  And supposing I was to suggest that I didn't take my Sky down to the club today? Suppose I was to pretend she'd got a touch of croup—and I wasn't entering her? What would you think about that?

CHARLIE. Are you serious?

FRED. I'm making an offer! Look—you clear this mess up—I'll pay for it—and promise to keep your mouth shut—and I'll promise not to take Sky and enter her. What do you say?

CHARLIE. Can I have it in black and white?

FRED. You can have it in technicolor if you like!

CHARLIE (*rising*)  All right—it's a deal!

(CHARLIE *moves* C *towards Fred and automatically sticks out his hand to shake on the bargain.* FRED *does the same. Before their hands meet, they both seem to realize, and rather shamefacedly withdraw*)

I'm sorry. I was forgetting myself.

FRED (*crossing behind him towards the sideboard*)  Yes—it's not as serious as all that!

CHARLIE (*returning to the settee and sitting*)  Look! You let me have it in writing—and then let's hear what you want me to do.

FRED (*collecting a pen and writing pad from the sideboard, and going to sit* L *of the table*)  All right, you can have it in writing. They used to call me the barrack-room lawyer!

CHARLIE. I can believe that!

FRED (*reading aloud, as he writes*)  I, Fred Furnival, do hereby promise Charlie Gibbs, that in return for services rendered by the old fathead Charlie Gibbs . . .

CHARLIE (*rising indignantly*)  The *what!*

FRED (*scratching out*)  Sorry! A slip of the pen.

(CHARLIE *sits down again*)

(*Continuing writing*) By the *aforesaid* Charlie Gibbs—I will not take Furnival Skyranger to the club secretary and enter her for the Cross-Channel Race—Signed . . .

CHARLIE (*quickly*)  Hey! Wait a minute. What about witnesses?

FRED.  Witnesses! You don't want anybody else to know about this?

CHARLIE.  It's only your signature they witness.

FRED (*hurt*)  So you don't trust me? All right. (*Calling*) Cissie! Emma!

(CISSIE *enters* R)

(*To Cissie*)  Come over here.

(CISSIE *crosses* R *of the table.*
EMMA *enters from the stairs and moves* R *of Cissie*)

(*Pushing the pad across the table*)  That's my signature. I want you two to witness it.

(CISSIE *signs and passes the pen to Emma*)

EMMA (*as she signs*)  What have you been buying now?

FRED.  Peace of mind! (*Receiving back the pad, he rips off the sheet and brings it down to Charlie*) There! The last will and testament of Fred Furnival.

CHARLIE (*rising and taking it*)  And Furnival Skyranger!

(FRED *moves down* R)

CISSIE (*to Charlie*)  Can we start clearing up?

CHARLIE.  It depends on your father.

CISSIE.  Dad! Can we . . . ?

FRED.  Emma! Send that lad in.

EMMA.  Which lad?

CHARLIE.  My apprentice. He's minding the cart outside.

FRED (*to Emma*)  And you stop out there, and watch for Gladys coming back.

(EMMA *exits* L. CISSIE *sits in the armchair* R)

(*To Charlie*)  Now! What's that lad's name?

CHARLIE.  Watson, Willie Watson.

FRED.  Are you prepared to give him a day off?

CHARLIE.  It's not in the bargain!

FRED (*crossing to Charlie and snatching the paper from his hand*)  All right! We'd better rip this up! (*He makes as though to tear it in half*)

CHARLIE (*anxiously*)  Now, now! I never said I wouldn't.

FRED.  You'll give him a day off?

CHARLIE.  I will. But not a second more!

FRED.  Good! (*He hands the agreement back to* CHARLIE, *who puts it in his inside pocket*)

(WILLIE WATSON *enters* L)

CHARLIE (*down* L *in front of the settee*)  Ah, there you are, Willie! Come here.

WILLIE (*coming down* C *in front of the table*)  It wasn't me, Mr Gibbs—I never touched nothing.

FRED (R *of Willie*)  No—but you're going to! How would you like a ten-shilling note?

WILLIE.  I'd sooner have a pound!

CHARLIE.  And a day off as well?

WILLIE (*knowingly*)  What's she going to ask me?

CHARLIE.  Who?

WILLIE.  Your missus? Would it be that blonde barmaid when we were doing *The Rose and Crown?*

CHARLIE (*annoyed*)  I'll do *you* in a minute!

FRED.  Willie! Do you want to earn ten bob and a day off?

(CHARLIE *sits on the settee*)

WILLIE.  You bet! What to do?

FRED.  Act!

WILLIE.  In a play?

FRED.  No.

WILLIE.  Well, if it's a musical—my voice wants mendin'!

FRED.  Look! Go out there and stand by the handcart . . .

(WILLIE *shoots off towards the door* L)

(*Bawling*) Come back! There's more than that!

WILLIE (*returning* C *front of the table*)  I thought there'd be a catch in it.

FRED.  You stand by the handcart and start crying. If anybody speaks to you—don't answer! Just go on crying! When I call you in—stop crying and say "Yes" to everything. Got it?

WILLIE.  I think so. Can you lend me a hanky?

FRED (*moving to Willie, taking out a handkerchief*)  Here you are— you can cry into that.

WILLIE (*scornfully*)  Don't be cissy! There won't be any tears.

CHARLIE.  Then what's the hanky for?

WILLIE.  To wipe this paint off my fingers!

FRED (*snatching back the handkerchief, and moving down* R)  Off you go and start crying!

WILLIE (*standing his ground*)  What about the deposit?

FRED (*turning to Willie*)  Which deposit?

WILLIE (*sticking out his hand*)  Fifty per cent! Five bob on account.

CHARLIE (*to Fred*)  I could have warned you about him!

FRED (*giving Willie two half-crowns*)  All right.

WILLIE.  Thanks. (*Pointing to Charlie*) Is *he* in on this?

FRED.  He is.

WILLIE (*indicating Cissie*)  Her, too?

FRED.  Yes.

WILLIE (*giving Charlie a wink accompanied by a cheeky shake of the head*) O.K., pal! (*Repeating the wink and gesture to Cissie*) O.K.,

toots! (*He moves towards the door* L *then turns and faces the others*)
How's this? (*He pretends to wipe the smile off his face with his right
hand, then draws his left hand over his face. As the hand passes, his face
creases up, and he begins to emit a continuous yowl. He turns and disappears through the door* L)

FRED.  You needn't make all that din! And tell Mrs Derbyshire
she can come back now.

CHARLIE (*rising*)  Well—what happens now?

FRED.  We start clearing up.

CISSIE (*rising*)  Thank goodness!

    (CISSIE *and* CHARLIE *begin collecting loose wallpaper from the
floor*)

FRED.  Not too fast! I said *start*.

CHARLIE.  But Gladys'll be back any minute.

FRED.  The sooner the better.

CHARLIE.  Look here—it's about time you explained what
you're . . .

    (EMMA *enters in a fluster* L)

EMMA (*coming* C, L *of the table*)  She's here—Gladys—she's
coming!

FRED.  All right—keep calm! How far away is she?

EMMA.  Right outside. (*To Charlie*) She's talking to that boy
of yours.

FRED.  That's fine! Now—everybody to work—and leave the
talking to me.

    (*All four start collecting up wallpaper from the floor. They do not
take down any from the walls.* FRED *is down* R. EMMA, *up* R. CISSIE
*and* CHARLIE *are up* L. GLADY'S *voice is heard off* L)

GLADYS (*off*)  Well, if *you* won't tell me—I'll find someone who
will!

    (GLADYS, *in hat and coat, enters* L)

(*As she enters*)  What's this lad crying for?

FRED.  You might well ask. Just look at this!

    (GLADYS *stops* C *and stares in speechless amazement*)

GLADYS. (*crossing and dropping into the armchair* R)  What have
they taken?

FRED (*down* R)  Who?

GLADYS.  The burglars.

FRED.  There's only one person had a hand in this, Gladys.

GLADYS.  You mean they've *got* him?

FRED.  *We've* got him!

    (CHARLIE *moves behind the settee,* EMMA *behind the armchair,* R)

FRED. I think you'd better see him. (*Crossing to the door* L *and calling*) Willie! (*Returning down* L *to the end of the settee*) You're in for a surprise, Gladys—and a shock!

(WILLIE *enters, moving down* C *in front of the table. He rubs his knuckles in his eyes*)

(*To Willie*) Well—what have you got to say for yourself?
WILLIE. Yes!
FRED. I mean . . .
GLADYS. Has that boy let him get away?
WILLIE. Yes!
FRED (*quickly*) No! (*To Willie*) Shut up! (*To Gladys*) Listen, Gladys—I'm going to ask this lad a few questions. Just you take notice of the answers. (*To Willie*) You came to this house early on this morning, didn't you?
WILLIE. Yes!
FRED. You were fed up watching Mr Gibbs hang paper—and you wanted to try yourself, didn't you?
WILLIE. Yes!
FRED. How did you get in?
WILLIE. Yes!
FRED (*hastily*) I mean—you found the front door open, didn't you?
WILLIE. Yes!
GLADYS (*to Fred*) What did I tell you about locking up?
FRED. That'd be Joe—going out.
EMMA (*moving down* R) Oh, no—it wasn't!
FRED (*to Emma*) It doesn't matter—does it?
WILLIE. Yes!
FRED (*angrily*) Shut up! And this is the horrible result of your first attempt at decorating—isn't it. *You've* done this—haven't you?
WILLIE (*forgetting his part*) I say! That's a bit thick! It's worth more than ten . . . !
FRED (*shouting him down*) *Shut up!* (*Continuing as before*) This is *your* handiwork—isn't it?
WILLIE (*sullenly*) Yes!
FRED (*to Gladys*) There you are, see! Now—are you going to prosecute?
GLADYS. What's Charlie going to do?

(FRED *indicates "sacking" to Charlie with a kick of his foot*)

CHARLIE (*nodding to Fred*) I'll show you! Willie!
WILLIE. Yes?
CHARLIE. Go back to the shop—draw your money and your cards—you're sacked!

(GLADYS *leans forward and shakes her head*)

WILLIE (*indignantly*) What! For ten measly bob?

CHARLIE. That's enough! Wait for me outside.

WILLIE (*winking at Charlie*) O.K.!

(*Turning to Fred so that Gladys can't see him,* WILLIE *gives a wink and thumbs up sign, then sets up a howl and exits* L)

FRED (*moving to Gladys, down* C) Well—what do you say? Are you going to take action as well?

GLADYS. What do you think?

FRED. Well—he's only a kid! I might have done the same thing myself once! I reckon he's been punished enough.

GLADYS. So do I. But I can't think what came over him. (*Rising*) Anyway, I'm not going to sit looking at this all day. (*Moving up* R)

CHARLIE. Don't worry. I'll go and bring the other lad. I'll soon have it put to rights.

GLADYS. You'd better! (*At the foot of the stairs*) I must say it appears to have done one good thing.

FRED. What's that?

GLADYS. It's brought you two closer together. If I were you— I'd stay that way!

(*She exits up the stairs*)

FRED (*to Charlie*) Yes—I reckon we'll both have to be pretty close over this lot!

CHARLIE. Is she likely to come back.

FRED. Not her—it's Saturday morning.

CHARLIE. What does that mean? (*Moving down* L *below the settee*)

FRED. Bed-changing! (*Suddenly realizing*) Emma! Cissie! Get up there before she comes out of the bathroom!

CISSIE. What for?

FRED. The bed! Rumple the clothes up!

EMMA. Oh dear! I'd forgotten!

(CISSIE *and* EMMA *rush off up the stairs* R)

FRED (*moving up* R *to the bottom of the stairs and shouting after them*) And throw my 'jama trousers under the dressing table! (*Moving down back* C *to Charlie*) Phew! That was a close shave?

CHARLIE (*indicating the door* L) Shall I bring him in?

(WILLIE *enters* L)

WILLIE. You don't need. I've never been out! (*Moving to the* L *of Fred*) Ten shillings, please? I'll take a note!

FRED. You will not! (*Offering some coins*) Here's the other five bob!

WILLIE (*pushing it away*) Ten shillings—or nothing!

FRED. All right—*nothing!*

WILLIE.  It better hadn't be!

FRED.  But you agreed to ten shillings?

WILLIE.  An' I was promised a ten-shilling note. I haven't had it!

CHARLIE.  It's blackmail, but I don't see what else you can do.

FRED.  All right! But it's the last thing he'll ever get out of me. Here! (*Handing over a note*)

WILLIE.  Thanks.

CHARLIE.  Now clear out—and take the day off.

WILLIE.  You mean the rest of the day! I'll take the balance on Monday.

CHARLIE.  You'll take a belt over the ear if you don't disappear quick!

WILLIE (*cheekily*)  O.K.! (*Moving towards the door L, then turning*) By the way, Mr Furnival—can I get a couple of ice lollies?

FRED.  You can get what you like. The shop's just across the road.

WILLIE.  No, thanks. I'd rather have yours. I don't have to pay for them. Ta-ta!

(WILLIE *exits* L)

FRED.  What is he talking about?

CHARLIE.  I haven't the slightest idea. (*Moving* C *to Fred*) Well— I hope you're satisfied?

FRED.  I'm satisfied of one thing.

CHARLIE.  What's that?

FRED.  I'm hand in glove with the two biggest rogues in Prestfield!

CHARLIE.  Yes—and they're in partnership with the biggest liar! (*Moving slightly up* L) Well, I'll go and find the other lad. And when I get back . . .

FRED.  Yes?

CHARLIE.  I'll be grateful if you're somewhere else. I don't want *you* sittin' watching me!

FRED.  Don't worry. When I study still life—I go to the art gallery.

CHARLIE.  Bah! (*He goes to the door* L)

(*As* CHARLIE *gets to the door* JOE *enters*)

And *bah* to you, too—you little lap-dog!

(CHARLIE *pushes Joe roughly out of the way and exits* L. JOE *turns and watches him go; then puts his hand over his eyes and moves a step or two towards the table*)

FRED.  And what are you supposed to be—one of the three Chinese monkeys? Open your eyes!

JOE.  I daresn't.

FRED.  Why not?

JOE. I had a funny dream last night. I'm frightened of what I might see.

FRED. You'll see it all right. Open 'em up!

(JOE *opens his fingers and peeps around the room*)

Well? Has it broken your dream?

JOE. It's broken my nerve!

(FRED *sits in the armchair* R *nursing his head*)

FRED. Oh—this head o' mine! It's opening and shutting!

JOE (*moving down* C, L *of Fred*) What did she hit you with?

FRED (*angrily*) Nothing! And don't waste sympathy on me! What about *you?* Not turning up for work?

JOE. But I did go to work!

FRED. Then you've got the sack!

JOE. I've got a pound a week *rise!*

FRED. *What?*

JOE. A pound a week rise!

FRED. What for?

JOE. Well, I woke up about two o'clock and found myself on that settee. Come to think of it—I'd got a nasty head, too!

FRED. Throbbing?

JOE. No—just nasty! (*Rubbing his hand through his hair*) Anyway, I spoke to you but you didn't seem to take any notice.

FRED. I was asleep.

JOE. No! You were sticking little bits of wallpaper on your chest and saying: "Look—I'm a stamp album!" My—but it was a good job I was late!

FRED. Why?

JOE. Just by the main gate—I saw a couple of chaps nip over the wall. I phoned the police from a call-box—and they caught 'em. The police sent for the boss—he overlooked me being late—and promised me the rise!

FRED. Well, I'll be . . . !

JOE. The boss even said something about a medal. Do you think they'll give me a medal?

FRED. If they do—it'll be a poor substitute for the Cross-Channel Cup!

JOE. What do you mean?

FRED. We've lost it!

JOE. Lost it? The race hasn't started yet!

FRED. Listen! To get myself out of this mess and keep Gladys in the dark—I've promised Charlie Gibbs I won't enter Sky.

JOE. You've *what?* (*He moves to the settee down* L)

FRED. Promised I wouldn't enter Sky. I've even put it in writing.

JOE. What were the words you used? (*He sits on the upstage end of the settee*)

FRED. "I will not take my bird Furnival Skyranger to the club secretary and enter her".

JOE. Well! It's simple.

FRED. What's simple?

JOE. *You've* promised not to take her—so *you* won't! But if *I* take her and enter her in *your* name . . . ?

(FRED *moves to the settee to shake Joe's hand.* JOE *rises to accept the handshake*)

FRED (*delighted*) Joe! If your firm don't give you a medal—I will! *And* it'll have a coat of arms!

JOE. What will it be?

FRED. Two brothers-in-law rampant, over one paper-hanger recumbent!

JOE (*suddenly serious*) Fred! Charlie Gibbs said I was a lap-dog. (*He moves down* L *and sits on the end of the settee*)

FRED. Don't let it upset you.

JOE. But I am upset! He's likened me to a pekinese! What should I do about it?

FRED. Stop snufflin' and get your hair cut! Anyway, there's no time to lose. (*Going to the upstage end of the settee to the sideboard*) The birds have got to be down at the club before noon. (*He picks up the pigeon-basket and moves back down* C *in front of the table*) Here's the box. We'll go and get Sky. Now—here's what I want you to do . . .

(WILLIE *appears furtively through the door* L)

WILLIE. Hey! Mr Furnival!

FRED. Well?

WILLIE. Can I have half a dozen choc ices? I want to treat some pals.

FRED. As long as you keep away from here, you can have what you want! Go on—hop it!

WILLIE. Thanks a lot. You're a sport!

(WILLIE *vanishes* L)

JOE. What's the matter with him?

FRED. I'm blest if I know! (*Moving towards the door* L) Anyhow, come on!

(JOE *rises*)

Here's the money for the entrance fee. All you've got to do is hand Sky over—get a receipt—and come straight back. It shouldn't take a couple of minutes. Turn right at the first corner—it's number twenty-seven on the left-hand side, and . . .

(*During his last sentence* FRED *and* JOE *disappear through the door* L. FRED *pushing Joe before him. Their voices die away.*

D

CISSIE *enters from the stairs* R, *she is carrying some roughly folded sheets. She deposits them on the table, just as someone knocks at the door* R. *She goes to the foot of the stairs and calls up*)

CISSIE. Mum! He's here—the laundryman! Where's the book?
GLADYS (*off* R)  In the kitchen!
CISSIE (*crossing to the door* R *and opening it*)  You'll have to wait a minute. It's not . . . (*Catching sight of the person outside*) Oh! It's you! (*Coolly turning away and moving* C)

(PETER *enters* R *from the kitchen*)

PETER.  C-can I come in?
CISSIE (*with her back to him*)  If you want to see somebody—yes.
PETER.  Thank you, (*he swallows*) very much. (*He stands just inside the door, staring around the room*)
CISSIE (*over her shoulder*)  Well?
PETER.  It—it's a pretty paper, isn't it?
CISSIE.  Is that *all* you've got to say? Have you lost your tongue?
PETER (*miserably, moving down* R)  No—but I've lost a wife.
CISSIE.  In that case you've come to the wrong place. The police-station's lower down.
PETER (*getting worked up*)  Look! You know jolly well what I mean! And about last night—it wasn't my fault. I was just dragged in!
CISSIE (*turning to face him*)  Dragged in! Judging by the dirty grin on your face—you were carried away, too!
PETER (*warmly*)  I tell you I never . . .
CISSIE (*cutting him short*)  It's no use! I couldn't trust you after that. Come to think of it—I'm wondering if you *do* take those opera-glasses to the theatre to watch the drummer?
PETER (*getting really worked up*)  That's enough! It's time I put my foot down! Cissie!
CISSIE.  Well?
PETER (*gently, but firmly*)  Come over here, and—(*forcibly*) kiss me!
CISSIE.  What!
PETER (*gently, but determined*)  I said: "Come over here and kiss me!"
CISSIE.  How dare you! You—gorilla!
PETER (*slightly puzzled*)  Gorilla? Last night I was a caveman!
CISSIE.  That was before you let your hair down!
PETER.  All right! If that's how you want it—I'm a gorilla! (*He beats his fists on his chest, sets his face into a leer, hangs his arms down gorilla-wise, and begins a bow-legged shamble towards Cissie*)
CISSIE. (*getting alarmed*) Peter! Don't! Don't be silly! Stop it! (*She backs slightly vp* L)

(PETER, *still acting the gorilla, points suddenly to the door* L)

PETER (*roaring*)  A-a-a-a-ah!

(CISSIE *swings round to see who is there but, of course, there is no-one. Before she has time to recover* PETER *seizes her in his arms and kisses her*)

CISSIE (*coming to and opening her eyes*)  My caveman!

PETER.  No, I'm not! I'm a gorilla! I'm enjoying it, too! Let's do it again.

(PETER *walks down* R *to begin his performance again, he beats his chest.*

    *Suddenly* FRED *appears in the doorway* L. PETER *shambles forward and points to the door* L)

PETER (*blood-curdling*)  A-a-a-a-ah! (*He catches sight of Fred and his cry ends in a gurgle. He is petrified*)

(FRED *stands applauding*)

FRED.  Encore! Encore!

PETER.  I was just showing Cissie a—a . . .

FRED.  I know. Jolly good dance it is! (*Moving down* L *behind the settee*) What do you call it, the African Veleta?

CISSIE.  Peter was showing me a game he used to play as a boy. He'd just gone down into his childhood memories.

FRED.  If you ask me—he'd just gone up into his family tree! (*He sits on the downstage end of the settee*)

CISSIE.  Dad! (*She moves towards Fred*)  Isn't it about time we had that private little chat?

FRED.  What about?

CISSIE (*sitting on the upstage end of the settee*)  Now don't pretend! I can't imagine what hold you've got over Aunt Emma—but you've none over me!

FRED.  Do we have to discuss it in front of him? (*Pointing to Peter*)

CISSIE.  Don't be silly. He was here!

FRED.  He was! Doing what?

CISSIE.  We were practising.

FRED.  The "Tarzan act"?

CISSIE.  An elopement!

FRED (*rising and moving down* L)  Cissie! You'd never do that! You'd never run away?

CISSIE.  Unfortunately you grabbed him, and made him a technician.

FRED.  A technician?

CISSIE.  In your production of *The Seven Veils*.

FRED.  And what was he responsible for?

PETER.  Two veils—and a bit of the sound track!

FRED.  I see. Well—(*blustering again*)—one thing I'm *not* going to stand for! And that's any more of this eloping nonsense!

CISSIE (*rising*)  Neither are we! What do you say, Peter?

PETER.  Rather! The next ladders I play with will be printed on a board—*and* the snakes!

CISSIE (*moving towards Peter*)  Don't you call dad and Uncle Joe snakes!

FRED.  Anyway—what's all this leading up to?

CISSIE (*coming back to the upstage end of the settee*)  Simply that you're going to give your consent to Peter and I getting married in the proper way.

FRED.  Oh, no, I'm not! (*He sits on the downstage end of the settee*)

CISSIE (*sitting beside him*)  Oh, yes, you *are!*

FRED.  But don't you see—it wouldn't be any use.

CISSIE.  Why not?

FRED.  Because *his* father would never agree.

PETER.  I'm afraid that's true.

CISSIE.  Nonsense! Don't forget we've got a hold over Mr Gibbs as well.

FRED.  What's that?

CISSIE.  All those lies he told mum about the apprentice lad.

FRED.  And supposing you told her the truth. Who would she go for—Charlie Gibbs, or me?

CISSIE.  I see what you mean. Very well—if we can't threaten, we'll have to get round him some other way. Can we tell him that *you've* no objection?

FRED.  You can if you like.

PETER.  Thanks very much, Mr Furnival.

FRED.  Don't thank me. *I* haven't done anything!

CISSIE.  Oh, yes, you have! You've given your consent!

FRED.  All I've said is—if his father agrees—then I'll consider it. I think that's a fair risk?

CISSIE (*rising and moving towards the door* L)  In that case we'd better get started. Come on, Peter!

PETER (*moving up* L)  Where are we going?

CISSIE.  To find your father.

FRED.  There's no need. He'll be back here soon.

CISSIE.  And he'll be too busy to bother with us! No—we're going to tackle him now. Come along!

(CISSIE *goes off through the door* L)

FRED.  And I wish you joy!

PETER (*just about to follow Cissie*)  Pardon?

FRED.  I said: "I wish you luck!"

PETER.  Thanks. (*Coming back to* L *of the table*)  Oh—Mr Furnival?

FRED.  Yes?

PETER.  I wonder if you'd mind if I called . . .

FRED.  Not at all! Call whenever you like.

PETER.  No—it isn't that. It's something between you and me.

FRED.  Well—out with it!

PETER. Now that we understand one another better—I'd like to treat you like I treat my own father. May I?

FRED. Certainly.

PETER (*moving up* L *to the door*) That's wonderful! Goodbye—Pop!

FRED (*rising angrily*) *Pop?*

(*But* PETER *has vanished after Cissie.*
*A head appears round the door* R, *it is* JOE. *He carries a pigeon clock*)

JOE. Have they gone?

FRED. Yes. On a wild-goose chase, too—if they only knew it.

JOE (*moving to* L *of the armchair*) Have you been making more promises?

FRED. Promises—Joe—are like pie-crusts. Some melt in the mouth. Others lie on the stomach!

JOE. So you've consented, eh? Well—you know what women are. They sit on your knee—twist your hair—breathe down your collar . . .

FRED. —and stick a gun in your back! But she'll find out what she's up against if she fires at Charlie. He's got armour-plated skin! (*Moving up* C *towards Joe*) Well, come on—you haven't told me!

JOE. Told you what?

FRED. About Sky. You got her in all right?

JOE. Oh, yes—she's entered. And they've sent your clock—here it is. (*Handing over the clock*) He says something about it being checked and set.

(FRED *takes the clock and puts it on the sideboard*)

(*Sitting in the armchair* R) Are you going to tell *Gladys* that you agree to the youngsters getting married?

FRED (*turning from the sideboard*) Not me! That would be an about-face. Gladys wouldn't half be suspicious! (*Moving below the settee down* L) But just in case those kids manage to get round Charlie—*somebody* had better get her used to the idea.

JOE. Who?

FRED. You!

JOE. *Me?*

FRED. Yes. (*He sits on the downstage end of the settee*) You can drop a hint or two that they ought to be settling down. Tell her you believe you can talk me round. Tell her they're so in love with one another that the wedding's bound to take place sooner or later.

JOE. You expect *me*—to say all—*that?*

FRED. Why not?

JOE. Couldn't you write it down?

FRED. I've put enough on paper for one day!

JOE. Well—if you're sure—I'll do my best.

(WILLIE WATSON *appears through the door* L *again. He has a block of ice-cream in each hand, and licks them alternately*)

WILLIE (*coming to the top of the settee,* L *of the table*)  Hey—Mr Furnival!

FRED.  Well?

WILLIE.  They're smashing! You won't mind if I have a few more, will you?

FRED (*rising; angrily*)  I thought I told you to keep away!

WILLIE.  You did! But if I'm going to ask permission . . . ?

FRED.  Look! You can fill yourself up to there—(*hand on chin*)— stick your Adam's apple on top—and call yourself a fruit sundae, for all I care! But don't let it bring you anywhere near this house!

WILLIE.  That's a bit difficult, Mr Furnival—but I'll try. Ta-ta!

(WILLIE *disappears again* L)

JOE.  Something's bothering that lad. Do you think it's his conscience?

FRED.  It isn't his stomach!

(*The voices of* EMMA *and* GLADYS *are heard approaching from the stairs*)

JOE.  Look out—they're coming!

FRED (*sitting on the downstage end of the settee*)  Right. Here's where you start your propaganda.

JOE.  What about?

FRED.  Those two love-birds—Cissie and the Weasel.

JOE.  Weasel! Why weasel?

FRED.  You wait till you hear him go "Pop!"

(GLADYS *enters talking to* EMMA. *She carries pillow-cases and moves up* C, *behind the table*)

GLADYS (*as she enters*)  So I went in to see the doctor. As soon as I opened the door he looked at me and said . . . (*Talking to Fred*) My goodness—you've not shaved!

FRED (*to Gladys*)  I didn't know you did.

GLADYS.  Not me—*you!*

(EMMA *exits to the kitchen* R)

FRED (*rubbing his hand over his chin*)  Oh, this? It won't take a minute. I've only got to pull a razor over my face.

GLADYS.  Then mind your eyelids! They're sticking out like shop-window blinds! Are you ill or something?

FRED.  Not me! I never felt better.

GLADYS.  You never looked worse! Off you go and tidy yourself up.

FRED (*crossing towards the stairs*)  All right. (*To Joe, in passing*)

Don't forget what I told you, Joe! (*To Gladys*) And when I come down I'll try a cup of weak tea.

GLADYS. You'll have your breakfast like everybody else.

FRED (*at the foot of the stairs*) Breakfast? (*He grimaces*)

GLADYS. There's a bit of fatty bacon?

FRED (*screwing up his eyes*) Not for me!

GLADYS (*busy bundling up the laundry*) Egg on toast, then?

FRED. No, thanks!

GLADYS. All right—what will you have?

FRED (*on the top step*) Two aspirins on a digestive biscuit!

> (FRED *disappears up the stairs.*
>
> EMMA *enters* R *with the laundry book and string. She moves up* C *to* R *of Gladys*)

GLADYS (*to Emma*) I knew this would happen. He's always the same when he's had too many peppermints. They do upset his stomach! (*To Joe*) You're not looking so clever either!

JOE (*who is just lighting his pipe*) Oh! I'm fine! (*He rises and moves down* R)

EMMA (*slyly*) He had a most peaceful night at the warehouse—hadn't you, Joe?

JOE (*uneasily*) Y-yes—I did.

EMMA. They rely on him, you know. I can't think whatever they'd do if he was ill and couldn't turn up!

JOE (*playing up*) That's right. (*Crossing to the left end of the settee and sitting*) I've gone many a time when I wasn't fit.

EMMA. Like last night! (*Moving* R *with the laundry bundle which she and Gladys have now made up between them*) I wouldn't have been surprised if he'd stopped off!

> (EMMA *exits with the bundle* R)

JOE. Well, you know how it is—you can't let them down.

GLADYS (*moving down towards Joe*) What was the matter with you?

JOE. I—er—I'd got something on my mind.

GLADYS. What?

JOE. About Cissie.

GLADYS. Cissie? What's she been doing?

> (EMMA *re-enters without the bundle and moves to the armchair*)

JOE. Oh, nothing—really.

GLADYS (*to Emma*) Isn't that just like a man! He either says too much or too little! Come on—out with it! What's up?

JOE. Well, if you must know—I don't like to see young people unhappy!

GLADYS. Who's unhappy?

JOE. Cissie and Peter.

(*Unseen by the others,* Fred *appears at the top of the stairs. He has a towel round his neck, and is lathering his face briskly with a shaving brush*)

Gladys. And what's making them unhappy?

Joe. Getting married!

Gladys. Is that all? Well, I hope they don't go bothering Fred about it—or they'll be more unhappy still!

Joe. I shouldn't run away with that idea—if I were you. Fred might not be as much against it as you think. I've been talking to him myself—quietly!

Gladys. I'll bet he didn't answer quietly!

Joe. It's too serious for mockery, Gladys. As a matter of fact—having got over the first shock—I think Fred's quite prepared to be reasonable.

Gladys. Serious? Shock? Look here—what are you driving at?

Joe. Don't you realize the wedding's *bound* to take place sooner or later?

Gladys (*slightly alarmed*) *Bound* to?

Joe. It's *got* to!

Gladys (*more alarmed*) Really?

Joe. Of course! They've *got* to get married!

Gladys. *Got to? My Cissie? Oh!*

(Gladys *bursts into tears, crying loudly. She turns to* Emma, *who comforts her.* Fred, *up aloft, is hopping about and shaking his fist at* Joe)

Emma (*to* Joe) You clumsy fool, you!

(Joe *rises, astonished*)

If you had to break the bad news—why couldn't you do it properly! (*To Gladys*) Come along, love—I'll get you a cup of tea.

(Emma *leads* Gladys *off* R *to the kitchen.* Fred *comes tearing downstairs to* Joe)

Joe (*gaping*) Bad news? What's she talking about?

Fred. You idiot! Why did you want to mess everything up like that?

Joe. But I've done nothing.

Fred. You told her they'd *got* to get married—didn't you?

Joe. Yes.

Fred. And don't you realize what she thinks?

Joe (*realization slowly dawning*) Oh—heck! (*He puts a hand to his mouth*)

(Joe *sits on the downstage end of the settee.* Fred *moves down* R)

JOE. Well, it's your fault! If you'd written it down—I wouldn't have been in trouble.

FRED (*turning to Joe*) Neither would somebody else!

(*Angry voices are heard outside the door* L)

CHARLIE (*off* L) Where is he? I'll soon settle this!

(CHARLIE GIBBS *enters* L *followed by* CISSIE *and* PETER. CHARLIE *is in a temper. He moves down* C. CISSIE *and* PETER *move behind the settee*)

CHARLIE (*moving down* R *to Fred*) Ah! there you are. Now—what's all this damned nonsense about these two?

FRED (*pointing to the lather on his face*) Where's your manners? Can't you see I'm in the middle of my toilet?

CHARLIE. I don't care if you're in the middle of a slipper-bath! I'm not having *my* family linked up with your lot!

FRED. *Your* family! I like that! How far back can you go?

CHARLIE. There was a Gibbs at Waterloo! There was a Gibbs in the Black Hole of Calcutta!

FRED. What was he doing—selling glow-worms?

(JIM DOBSON, *in uniform, enters* L)

CHARLIE. Look! I don't care what you told these two! I'm not going to . . .

JIM (*butting in*) Excuse me! (*Moving up* C) I'd like a word with one or two people here.

CHARLIE (*turning to Jim*) Am I included?

JIM. No.

CHARLIE. In that case I'll go. (*He turns to Fred*) And don't forget —we've got a bargain all right—but marriage *doesn't* enter into it!

(JIM *moves down* C)

FRED. All right—Pop! (*He dabs the shaving brush on Charlie's nose*)

CHARLIE. *What!*

JIM. I reckon you'd better get along. Come on—get moving!

(CHARLIE *exits* L *indignantly.* FRED *puts the brush down and starts mopping the lather off his face with the towel which he removes from around his neck*)

CISSIE (*to Jim*) Will you be wanting us—Peter and me?

JIM. I doubt it, Missy. My business concerns your father—*and* something that happened last night!

CISSIE. In that case we'll certainly stop!

JIM. As you please. But remember—no interference! (*He turns to Fred*) Now—if you're ready?

FRED. What's all this about?

JIM. A bicycle! *Your* bicycle!

FRED (*sarcastically*) Don't tell me it's obstructing the highway again!

JIM. All I want to know is—have you got it?

FRED. Got it? Certainly! It's out there in the shed.

JIM (*smugly*) Is it? (*He moves up* L *to the door*) Then how do you account for this?

(JIM *goes through the door* L *and reappears wheeling the selfsame bicycle that we saw in Act I. He wheels it over and props it against the armchair* R)

FRED. Here! Who gave you permission to fetch that out?

JIM. I've just wheeled this all the way from *The Bull and Butcher*. It's been standing outside there all night!

FRED (*taking the bicycle and putting it up* R *against the back wall*) Well, it's very kind of you—but there's no crime in that?

JIM. Maybe not! But I would like to know what vehicle you *did* bring home? You see *two* are reported "missing"!

FRED. Two?

JIM (*consulting his notebook*) One from a lock-up shed in the yard —the other from the lobby of *The Bull's* private quarters.

FRED. What's that got to do with me? I don't know anything about it!

JIM. Oh—you don't, don't you? Then it may interest you to know that I took the liberty of looking in your shed before I stepped in here?

FRED. And what did you find?

JIM. A small boy engaged in a felonious act—and *both* the missing vehicles!

FRED. I don't believe it!

JIM. Oh—you don't? (*He goes to the door* L *and opens it. Calling off*) Hey! You there! Bring on exhibit "A"!

(WILLIE WATSON *struggles in pushing an ice-cream vendor's bicycle, with a white container in front, labelled* TORNELLI—PURE ICES FRUIT LOLLIES. JIM *takes it over from* WILLIE *and props it against the front of the table*)

FRED (*eyes popping*) How in the name of heaven did that get here?

JIM. That's what I'd like to know! And that's not all! (*To Willie*) Go and fetch the other—exhibit "B"—and be quick!

(WILLIE *goes off* L *at the same time,* JOE *endeavours to sneak off, moving up behind the settee to the door* L. JIM *spots him*)

(*Calling to Joe*) Hey! Where do you think you're off to? Come back here!

(JOE *returns rather shamefacedly, and sits on the downstage end of the settee*)

Jim (*to Fred*) Mind you—I can understand you riding this one home—(*pointing to the ice-cream bicycle*)—but the other has me up a gum-tree! Tell me—(*he points dramatically towards the door* L)—why did you have to bring that as well?

(WILLIE *enters* L *wheeling a perambulator, with the hood up. He brings it down* C *then retires up* L)

FRED (*almost choking*) I never brought that thing!

JIM. Well, if *you* didn't—who *did?*

JOE (*after swallowing and gulping*) Me!

JIM (*turning on him*) Oh! So *you* brought it?

JOE. No. *It* brought me!

FRED. What the blazes are you talking about?

JOE. Don't you remember, Fred? You said you wouldn't see me walk while you were riding. So you made me sit in it—and gave me a tow with a clothes-line.

JIM. A clothes-line? That's another thing that's reported missing! Where is it?

FRED. I haven't the slightest idea. But I know where it ought to be!

JIM. Where?

FRED (*pointing at Joe*) Round his neck! (*To Jim*) Anyway, there's no harm done. You've got the things back! What are you going to do?

JIM. First—I'm going to return the property, and see if the people concerned wish to prefer a charge. Then—if they do—I'll be back to take statements from the three of you!

FRED. Three? There's only two of us!

JIM (*pointing to Willie*) And *him!* The felon! (*To Willie*) On second thoughts—you, my lad, can give a hand to get all this stuff back. I've got my own bicycle to cope with. Here—(*indicating the pram*)—you take this! I'll have to manage this—(*indicating the ice-cream bicycle*)—and my bike as well.

PETER. If it's any help, Mr Dobson—Cissie and I are going up that way. If you like—we'll take the pram for you?

JIM. Thanks very much! If you'll follow us on—I'll supervise this young rascal, and see he doesn't get his hands in any more. (*To Willie*) Come on—Crippen! Quick march!

(WILLIE *opens the door* L *for* JIM, *who guides the ice-cream bicycle backwards and out. They both exit*)

CISSIE (*moving round the settee to* C *in front of the table*) Well, Dad—you seem to have got around last night?

JOE. No wonder. He had a bicycle!

PETER (*moving* L *of Cissie*) There's no need to worry—Pop.

FRED. *Pop?* If you've something to say, lad—say it—don't keep blowing the cork out!

PETER. I'm sorry. I just wanted to tell you that Tornelli's a pal of mine. He won't make any bother.

FRED. Well—that's something.

JOE. And the pram belongs to my cousin at *The Bull*. He won't charge us—he'll just have a good laugh about it.

FRED. And his customers! I think I'd prefer to be charged! In camera—of course!

CISSIE. You can both be thankful mum and Aunt Emma know nothing about it. That saves you thinking up another fairy tale.

(*The voices of* EMMA *and* GLADYS *are heard off* R)

Only just in time, too! They seem to be coming back.

PETER (*pointing to the pram*) Hey! What about this?

FRED (*excitedly*) Get it out—quick! No, no—it's too late! Come here—all of you—and stand in front of it!

(PETER *has turned the pram pointing towards the audience. They all stand shoulder to shoulder in a line,* FRED *at the upstage end and* JOE *at the downstage end, with* CISSIE *and* PETER *in between.*
GLADYS *and* EMMA *enter* R *from the kitchen*)

GLADYS (*coming down*) Oh! Well, I'm glad you've had the sense to get everyone together. All right—let's get on with the meeting!

(GLADYS *sits in the armchair* R. EMMA *stands behind the armchair*)

FRED. Meeting? This isn't a meeting—it's—it's a rehearsal!

GLADYS. A rehearsal! What for?

FRED. The next Sunday School concert. We're singing a quartette!

GLADYS. What! Three male voices and one female?

FRED. That's all right. Joe's taking contralto! Ready, everybody? After three! One! Two! Three!

(FRED *begins to sing the first line of* "*Sweet and Low*", *the others quickly join in*)

GLADYS (*rising*) That's enough of that nonsense! What are you trying to hide?

FRED. Nothing. Nothing at all!

GLADYS. Come on. Stand apart—all of you!

(*Slowly they separate, revealing the pram*)

(*Shocked; pointing at the pram*) What is the meaning of this?

FRED. Well—I—er . . .

(FRED *goes upstairs* R)

CISSIE (*crossing to Gladys*) Mum! You can't blame anybody else but me. It's all my fault—really it is!

GLADYS (*crying*) All *her* fault? All my Cissie's fault! O-o-oh! (*She breaks down completely*)

CISSIE. Look, Mum! Peter and I want to get married as soon as possible. I'm nineteen—he's twenty. You don't think it's too soon?

GLADYS (*looking up from her handkerchief*) Too soon? (*Pointing to the pram again*) It's too late!

*With a howl* GLADYS *collapses in the armchair* R *where she is comforted by* EMMA. FRED *and* JOE *force* PETER *and* CISSIE *to the pram handle and push them towards the door* L *as—*

*the* CURTAIN *falls*

# ACT III

Scene—*The same. The following Thursday.*

*When the* Curtain *rises the living-room of the Furnival home is in apple-*
*pie order. The* r *half of the set is now neatly decorated with the same*
*wallpaper as the* l *and all signs of the late decorating have disappeared.*
*All the furniture is in position, everything is neat and clean.* Emma *and*
Gladys *are sitting at opposite ends of the table,* Gladys *is* r *of the*
*table and* Emma *is* l. *They are just finishing a meal.*

Emma (*laying down her knife and fork*) Very tasty! As my father
used to say: "There's nothing to beat a young lamb chop—unless
it's two!"

Gladys. Considering he was my father as well—I could be
expected to have heard it before!

Emma. I'm sorry. It's just that my mind's on other things.

Gladys. I'm sorry, too, Emma! I didn't mean to be rude. (*She
sighs*) If only I knew where she was—I'd feel happier.

Emma (*sighing*) Me, too!

Gladys. To walk out like that without a word! I could have
understood it if I'd reproached her in any way. Naturally I was
upset—but I was willing to stand by her.

Emma. Don't you think it's about time we notified the police?
They find missing persons by the dozen.

Gladys (*tearfully, producing her handkerchief*) I don't *want* a
dozen. I just want my Cissie.

Emma. They say young Peter's still missing. If you ask me—
wherever we find Cissie—we'll find him as well. As the detectives
say: "Share-shay La Fam!"

Gladys. What's that?

Emma. It's French. I think it means: "Search the woman
first".

Gladys. Does it? Then I don't want to know any French
detectives!

Emma. Well—if you won't go to the police—how about an
advert in the agony column? You know: "Come home—all
forgiven!"

Gladys. I couldn't! Besides—*all* are *not* forgiven! Those men
of ours haven't had their full punishment yet!

Emma. I meant to ask you about that. Couldn't we let up a bit
now? It's been a lot of silent meals—five whole days!

Gladys. It's been an eye-opener!

Emma. How?

GLADYS. At the table. Fred's never passed so many things to me without being asked since we were on our honeymoon!

EMMA. But we need their help, Gladys. They might be able to find Cissie?

GLADYS. Not Fred! He can't find his own socks!

EMMA. Supposing we do find them—what will you do?

GLADYS. If they haven't done the right thing themselves—they'll go straight round to the registrar's!

EMMA. Wouldn't it look better if they were married first?

GLADYS. That's what they'd be going to the registrar for!

EMMA. Oh, yes! He does *both* jobs, doesn't he?

GLADYS (*shocked*) Emma!

(FRED'S *voice is heard singing off* R)

EMMA. Here he is. (*Rising*) I'd better get his . . .

GLADYS. Not you! Stay where you are.

(EMMA *sits again.*
        FRED *enters* R *from the kitchen and comes* C *behind the table. He is wearing his best suit and cap, and carries a bunch of flowers wrapped in paper*)

FRED (*jovially*) Well—back home again! Back to the little women! And what a busy morning I've had!

(EMMA *and* GLADYS *both turn their heads away from him, looking down stage*)

Anyway—I've brought you some flowers. (*Holding them in front of Gladys*) There—look at those! Aren't they lovely?

(GLADYS *ignores them*)

(*holding them in front of Emma*) Don't you think they're lovely, Emma?

(EMMA *ignores them.*
        JOE *enters through the door* R)

(*Turning to Joe*) All right. We'll ask his opinion. Joe! Look at those! What have *you* got to say about them?

JOE. They're all the same colour! (*Moving down* R *to the fireplace*)

FRED (*trying to keep his temper*) Yes! (*He moves* R *of the table to* C; *to Gladys*) Well now—where are you going to have them? (*There is a pause; he moves down* L) I said: "Where are you going to have them?"

(GLADYS *rises grimly, and walks towards Fred.* FRED *holds out the flowers to her with a smile on his face, but she walks in front of him, and crosses below the settee to the sideboard. His smile fades, as he turns to watch her. She takes a cut-glass vase from the top of the sideboard, and walks back towards Fred around the upstage end of the settee.*

*Once again* Fred's *face lights up, and he holds out the flowers towards her. Ignoring this, she bends and places the vase on the floor beside him, then straightens up, and walks sedately and impassively back to the table, where she resumes her seat*)

(*Swallowing his annoyance*) Yes—well, I suppose that's as good a place as any. What do you say, Joe? (*He puts the vase* c *then gets on his knees and starts sticking the flowers into the vase one by one. He looks up at Joe, who is staring miserably at Emma*)

(Emma *and* Gladys *now concentrate their gaze on the box-window*)

(*To* Joe) Here! Come and give a hand!

(Joe *moves down* c *to Fred.* Fred *hands him some of the flowers.* Joe *gets down on one knee and places one of the flowers in the vase without taking his eyes off Emma.* Fred *having placed all his, bends right down over the vase to smell them*)

You want to smell them, Gladys—they've a beautiful scent!

(Joe, *coming down with a second bloom, and still staring at Emma— sticks the end of the stalk in Fred's right ear*)

Here! What the . . . ! (*Straightening up, holding his ear*)
Joe. Oh! I—I'm sorry, Fred. Did I push it in?
Fred. Push it in? You nearly planted it! (*He snatches the flowers and slams them into the vase all higgledy-piggledy*) There you are! (*Brusquely*) Well—hadn't they better have some water? (*Getting no response from the womenfolk, he softens his tone*) Gladys love—don't you think they'd like a drink?

(Gladys *and* Emma *turn to look at one another.* Gladys *nods to Emma, and points to the water-jug standing on the table by Gladys' left elbow.* Emma *rises, crosses behind the table towards Gladys. She picks up the jug, and comes down* R *of Gladys towards the men. She comes round in front of Joe, on his* R)

Joe (*picking up the vase and holding it out towards her*) Thanks, love! I knew *you'd* . . .

(Emma *sets the jug down on the floor in front of him, then straightens up and walks between the two kneeling men. She gives them both a push, so that they overbalance backwards, and she walks back to her place and resumes her seat*)

(*Recovering himself to a kneeling position, and holding out the water-jug to Fred*) Fred!
Fred. Yes?
Joe. Will you be mother—and pour?

(Fred *angrily snatches the jug.* Joe *picks up the vase and holds it close to him; as* Fred *clumsily attempts to pour, he spills some of the water over Joe*)

Here—be careful!

FRED. It's my carpet! (*He rises and moves to the settee*)

JOE. And these are my trousers! Now, where shall I put them?

FRED (*placing the water-jug on the sideboard*) Where the girls can see them, of course!

JOE (*rising*) In that case—there's only one place for them!

(JOE *walks up* R *round to the back of the table, where* EMMA *and* GLADYS *are both looking towards the window. He plants the vase in the middle at the back of the table. Immediately* EMMA *and* GLADYS *turn their heads simultaneously down stage.* JOE *slides the vase up to the front edge of the table, whereupon they turn back to look at the window.* JOE *draws the vase back, and they look forward again.* JOE *tries a little rapid sliding back and forth, until tired of behaving like spectators at a tennis match,* EMMA *and* GLADYS *both put their hands under their chairs, and with a quick lift, turn square towards the audience, and bang down their chairs together*)

FRED (*down* L) It's no use, Joe! We don't understand the language of flowers.

JOE (*releasing the vase*) What do you mean?

FRED. We've bought the wrong kind. We want some that use the deaf and dumb alphabet! Well—talk or no talk—I'm hungry! Come on—let's join the ladies!

(FRED *moves up* L *to the back of the table and draws out the chair next to Emma.* JOE *draws out the one next to Gladys and* R *of Fred. They both sit facing the audience. As soon as they are seated,* GLADYS *and* EMMA *rise in unison. They lift their chairs together and turn them facing the table. They bang them down together and lift their dirty plates together.*

*Without a word they stalk out through the door* R, GLADYS *leading.* FRED *and* JOE *gazing sorrowfully after them*)

JOE (*after they have gone*) Did you see what they've had?

FRED. Lamb chops!

JOE. English—or frozen?

FRED. Do you mean the chops—or them?

JOE (*reflectively*) Five days of it! I wonder if they'll *ever* come round?

FRED. I don't know—but I've just about had a bellyful!

JOE. Then why don't you tell them where Cissie is?

FRED. Not likely! I'll sort this out in my own way. As soon as I've done that—and not before—I shall bring them back!

JOE. But why did you send Peter to stay at your brother's as well?

FRED. I was forced to! When I told Cissie she'd got to disappear for a few days—she refused point-blank unless he went as well.

E

JoE. And to think they're only a couple of miles away! Wouldn't Gladys be mad if she knew?

FRED. Considering she's called there twice this week without finding 'em—yes!

JoE. Well, the sooner you get it sorted out the better, because I'm . . .

(*The door* R *begins to open*)

FRED. Look out! They're coming back.

(GLADYS *enters, followed by* EMMA. *They are each carrying a plate.* GLADYS *sets her in front of Fred, and* EMMA *puts hers in front of Joe*)

(*Staring at his plate*) Here—what's this? I thought we were having lamb chops?

(GLADYS *and* EMMA *immediately snatch up the plates again, as though to take them back*)

(*Hurriedly*) All right—leave it! Leave it!

(*They put the plates down again, and without a word march off through the door* R)

JoE (*disgustedly, looking at his plate*) Of all things—beans on toast!

FRED (*pushing his plate forward*) If that's my dinner—I've had it!

JoE. I thought you were hungry?

FRED. Not *that* hungry!

JoE (*offering the sauce-boat*) If you put mint sauce on it—it might taste like lamb!

FRED. And if I stick a couple of feathers in it—it might look like a chicken! Don't talk daft! Do you fancy it?

JoE. No.

FRED. Then how about going into town, and calling at Atkinson's?

(*The door* L *opens and* CISSIE *peeps in*)

CISSIE. So that's where you are!

(FRED *rises panic-stricken. He rushes to the door* L, *pushes* CISSIE *out and shuts the door again. He holds his foot against it*)

FRED (*pointing to the door* R) Joe! Lock that door!

JoE (*over at the door* R) I can't!

(CISSIE *outside is banging on the door* L)

FRED. Why not?

JoE. The key's on the other side!

FRED. Then hold the handle!

JoE. Right—I've got it! (*He stands with his back to the door*)

FRED (*opening the door* L *and moving* C)  All right—all right! Stop it now and come inside!

(CISSIE *enters, moving down* L *to the sideboard, followed by* PETER, *who comes to the upstage end of the settee*)

Didn't I tell you not to set one foot outside that house?

CISSIE.  That's just the trouble. We're fed up! (*She puts her handbag down on the sideboard*)

FRED.  After *five* days! (*He starts to move down* R, *then turns to Cissie*) Do you realize I've been under the same roof as your mother for twenty-five years?

CISSIE.  And how would you like to spend all day peeping through a lace curtain to see who's coming?

PETER.  And all night sleeping with Uncle Ted? He snores like a pig!

CISSIE.  It's as bad as being in prison!

PETER.  And for something you haven't done!

CISSIE (*moving below the settee down* L) So we've made up our minds! Either you make things right with mum—or we "spill the beans!"

FRED.  All right! (*Moving up* C *to the table*) Go ahead! (*Picking up his plate from the table and bringing it down to Cissie*) And while you're at it—you can spill these as well!

CISSIE.  So you don't mind?

(PETER *moves over* L, *behind the settee*)

FRED.  About *these*—no! (*Returning the plate to the table*) But about the other business—you've got to wait till I've worked out my plan!

CISSIE.  Have you got one? (*She moves up to Fred*)

(JOE *moves slowly* C, R *of Fred*)

FRED.  Several. I'm just waiting my chance to select the right one and put it into operation. You've got to give me more time!

CISSIE.  What do you say, Peter?

PETER.  Well—I . . .

FRED (*turning* R *and finding Joe beside him*)  Hey—Horatius! Back to your bridge!

(JOE *moves back hurriedly to guard the door* R)

CISSIE.  All right. We'll give you a little more time. But this is the last night we spend under Uncle Ted's roof!

FRED.  We'll see about that. (*He tries to shepherd them up*) In the meantime, you get back there as fast as you can—and don't let anybody see you!

JOE (*at the door* R)  I think someone's coming!

FRED.  Come along! Off you go!

(FRED *bustles Cissie and Peter out through the door* L, CISSIE *forgetting her handbag.* FRED *closes the door behind them, then moves down* L *behind the settee*)

All right. You can leave it now.

JOE. It seems to be a false alarm. (*Playing with the door knob*) Hey—Fred! You know what? This door is locked!

FRED. It's what?

JOE. It's locked! On the other side!

FRED. Never mind. Get after those two and shepherd them round the back streets. You needn't go all the way. Tell Cissie to put her scarf round her face—and the lad to pull his cap well down.

JOE (*who has moved up* C *behind the table*) Tell the lad *what?*

FRED. To pull his cap well down!

JOE. Have you seen his ears?

FRED. Go on—be quick or you'll miss them!

(JOE *moves up to the door* L, *before he can reach it, the door opens.*
    CHARLIE GIBBS *comes briskly in, down to the* L *corner of the table*)

CHARLIE (*as he passes Joe*) Hello, Joe! Going out?

(JOE *backs to the back wall by the door* L, *looks Charlie up and down, then draws himself up to his full height*)

JOE (*proudly*) Lap-dog, yourself!

(JOE *exits* L *closing the door behind him*)

FRED (*still down* L *behind the settee*) Well?

CHARLIE. The front door *was* open!

FRED. So was the pantry window. You want to try *that* some time! (*Moving across down* C, *facing down* R)

CHARLIE. I've come because I've something to settle with you —something important!

FRED. So you *did* see them?

CHARLIE (*obviously puzzled*) See who?

FRED (*realizing his mistake*) Why—er—Gladys and Emma. They just went out.

CHARLIE. Did they? I didn't see anybody.

FRED. Thank goodness for that! (*Turning to Charlie*) Well— what's the business?

CHARLIE (*thrusting out an envelope towards Fred*) This!

FRED. What is it?

CHARLIE. The bill for the decorating.

FRED. Is that all?

CHARLIE. What did you expect—a summons?

FRED. That's what you'll need before *I* pay! And even then—I won't!

CHARLIE. Why not?

FRED. Because it wasn't personally incurred!

CHARLIE. But you said last Saturday morning . . .

FRED. Did I? Who heard me?

CHARLIE. I did!

FRED. Who else?

CHARLIE. All right, then—Gladys called me in. You can't get away from that! And you're responsible for your wife's debts.

FRED. I'm also responsible for her teeth—but the National Health paid for 'em!

CHARLIE (*turning down* L) I might have expected it! (*He turns back to Fred*) You never could keep a bargain! Not even in writing!

FRED (*nonchalantly*) Oh?

CHARLIE. I know all about you entering Sky—sending her with Joe. And all the rest of the dirty business! The club secretary told me.

FRED. What do you mean "dirty business"? There was no breach of contract!

CHARLIE. Oh, no! You're too clever for that! Such a nice slap in the eye for me, wasn't it?

FRED (*airily turning away down* R) If you want to take it that way.

CHARLIE. Well—I've got a slap in the eye for you!

FRED. Really?

CHARLIE. Yes! Tell me, has Sky come back from France yet?

FRED (*more interested*) No, why?

CHARLIE. Well, it may interest you to know that Bert Jones' bird got back half an hour ago!

FRED (*turning quickly to Charlie*) Never!

CHARLIE (*relishing this*) And that's not all! One of Tom Mellor's young birds arrived an hour ago!

FRED. I—I don't believe it!

CHARLIE (*getting louder*) And *that's* not all! You've heard of my Smokey—haven't you?

FRED. Go on! Don't torture me!

CHARLIE. Well—my Smokey clocked in—(*he looks at his watch*) —two hours and thirty-five minutes ago—exactly! I thought you'd like to know. I'm just on my way to the club with the clock. (*Moving above the settee to the sideboard*) I'll leave this for you. (*Putting the bill on the sideboard*) It'll help to console you in your disappointment! (*He moves up to the door* L, *then turns as though struck by an afterthought*) Furnival Skyranger? (*He laughs*) Champion Furnival Skyranger? Ah-ah-ah-ah!

(CHARLIE *bursts into a peal of sarcastic laughter, turns, and disappears through the door* L, *still laughing and leaving the door ajar*)

FRED (*recovering himself*) I'll show you! I'll have that clock examined! I'll . . .

(*As* FRED *makes to follow* CHARLIE, JIM DOBSON *enters* L *followed by* JOE)

JIM. Hallo! Hallo! More trouble?

FRED. There must be if you've arrived. (*He turns and moves down* R) What is it this time?

JIM (*moving down* C *to the front of the table*) I found him—(*he jerks his thumb towards Joe*)—along the road—so I brought him with me. I wanted to report on that business of last Friday night!

(JOE *moves down behind the settee, putting his bowler on the sideboard*)

FRED. Report on it—or *harp* on it?

JIM. No. I think we can bring it to a satisfactory conclusion—all parties being willing.

FRED. Well?

JIM. The owner of the ice-cream vehicle is willing to overlook it—providing restitution is made for the missing lollies and ice-cream.

FRED. All right—we'll pay! (*He moves to the armchair* R, *then turns facing down* R) What does it come to?

JIM (*consulting his notebook*) The amount in question is—one pound, six shillings, and threepence!

FRED (*turning quickly to Jim*) *What!*

JIM. One pound—six shillings—and—(*studying his notebook*)—threepence-*halfpenny!*

FRED. Is that all? (*He sits in the armchair* R)

JIM (*putting his notebook away*) Not quite! There's still the matter of the boy—Willie Watson. Would *you* like to charge him?

FRED. Yes!

JIM. What with?

FRED. A herd of elephants!

JIM. Well—if that's all—we can consider the matter closed! (*Moving towards the door* L) An interesting bit of investigation—if I may say so—but not very profitable.

FRED. What do you mean?

JIM (*turning and tracing imaginary chevrons on his sleeve*) No stripes for anybody!

FRED. That's where you're wrong! I've not settled with young Willie yet!

JIM. Oh! You've got another visitor waiting to see you outside.

FRED. Why didn't you bring him in?

JIM. It's not a "him"—it's a "her". Didn't seem to want to come in while I was here.

FRED. All right—(*he rises and moves down* R)—send *her* in!

JIM (*standing against the back wall, by the open door* L) You can come in now, missus. I'm on my way!

FRED (*to Joe*)  One pound six and threepence-ha'penny—in ice-cream! What has that kid got—a stomach or a "hump"?

JOE (*sitting on the downstage end of the settee*)  It's a wonder he didn't need a doctor?

FRED.  Or a plumber—with a blowlamp!

(*A pram begins to appear through the door L with the hood up*)

(*Spotting it, and pointing*)  Who's bringing that thing again?

(*As it enters the room, it is followed by MRS WATSON, Willie's mother, who is propelling it from behind. As soon as she has passed him, JIM DOBSON exits L, closing the door behind him. MRS WATSON brings the pram down c in front of the table*)

(*Pointing to the pram*)  Here! What do you call this?

MRS WATSON.  Clarence—my youngest! I never leave him outside.

FRED.  And who are you?

MRS WATSON.  I'm his mother!

FRED (*sarcastically*)  You surprise me! I should have taken you for his father!

MRS WATSON.  I'm not talking about Clarence—it's my other lad I've come about—Willie!

FRED.  Willie?

MRS WATSON.  Willie Watson! You know—he works for Charlie Gibbs.

FRED.  So you're Mrs Watson?

MRS WATSON.  That's right.

FRED (*preparing for battle*)  I'm pleased to meet—*you!*

MRS WATSON (*also preparing for battle*)  I'm glad! Because I'm not pleased to meet you!

FRED (*a little taken aback*)  You're not?

MRS WATSON.  You ought to be ashamed of yourself—a great grown man like you!

FRED.  *I* ought?

MRS WATSON.  Stuffing him up with ice-cream like that! Do you know he's been off work for four days? And all through you! You ought to have more sense!

FRED.  Well—of all the . . . !

MRS WATSON.  And me having to trail young Clarence and the pram all the way here. If I'd known, I'd have sent his father!

JOE.  I don't think you would.

MRS WATSON.  Why not?

JOE.  Because I happen to know his father's doin' six months!

MRS WATSON (*to Joe*)  Look! I'll thank you to mind your own interference!

FRED.  Wait a minute! Joe! (*Moving up R of the pram*) Take a look at that pram. Doesn't it remind you of something?

JOE. Remind me? I could have sworn it was the same one!

MRS WATSON. What's the matter with the pram?

FRED. I'm glad you've asked that question, missus—I'll show you! (*He kneels beside the pram and takes one of the wheels in his hands*) See this wheel?

MRS WATSON. Yes!

FRED. Watch! (*He pretends to waggle it from side to side*) See the play there, Joe?

JOE. I do indeed.

MRS WATSON. Is something wrong?

FRED. Wrong! Do you know this pram's a veritable death-trap?

MRS WATSON (*indignantly*) It's a Patterson's de-luxe coach-built!

FRED. I mean it's dangerous! At any moment that wheel's likely to come off. And if it does . . . ?

MRS WATSON. Yes?

FRED. It'll pitch young Clarence out right on his dummy!

MRS WATSON. Good gracious! I'll take it back to the shop this minute!

FRED (*rising*) And supposing it happened on the way? No, I can't let you take the risk!

MRS WATSON. What do you mean?

FRED. That wheel's got to be repaired before you leave here! (*To Joe*) Joe! You're an expert on prams!

JOE. Am I?

FRED. Now—don't be modest! You know very well we can put this right in a few minutes. Look here, Mrs Watson—if you'll leave it with us . . . ?

MRS WATSON. *Leave* it! Do you think I'm going to carry young Clarence all the way home?

FRED. Certainly not! You leave Clarence as well—he'll come to no harm.

MRS WATSON. But I don't understand why . . . ?

FRED. And while we're at it—you needn't worry about Willie losing those four days. I'm quite willing to make up his wages.

MRS WATSON. Well, that's very kind of you, I'm sure.

FRED. Don't mention it! Now—off you go!

MRS WATSON. But I've got nowhere *to* go! I may as well sit here and watch you. (*Sitting on the upstage end of the settee*)

FRED (*moving to her, and raising her*) Oh, no! You must have some shopping to do?

MRS WATSON. I've done it.

FRED. Not all of it! (*Turning down* C) There's some you don't even know about yet! (*Turning to Joe*) Joe!

JOE. Yes?

FRED. Give her a pound!

JOE. *What?*

Mrs Watson (*to Joe*)  He said, "Give me a pound". (*To Fred*) What's the matter with him? Is he a bit deaf?

Fred.  That's right. You see, Joe, Mrs Watson is going out to buy herself a new hat.

Joe (*producing a note from his wallet*)  Is she? (*He rises holding the note*)

Fred.  And when she gets back—the pram will be repaired and ready to wheel away! (*To Mrs Watson*) Now—what do you think about that?

Mrs Watson (*taking the note from Joe's hand*)  Thanks very much?

(Joe *sits down again*)

(*To Fred*) You know, I've changed my mind about you, Mr Furnival. I've heard many a one say you weren't fit to burn—but I reckon you are!

Fred.  Yes, well off you go! There's a good woman! (*Almost pushing her off towards the door* L)

Mrs Watson (*stopping and turning short of the door*)  That's a funny thing, that is!

Fred.  What?

Mrs Watson.  It's the first time anyone's called *me* "a good woman" without getting their face scratched! (*She laughs*) Ah well—toodle-oo! I won't be long!

(Mrs Watson *exits* L)

Fred (*calling after her*)  That's all right. Don't hurry!

Joe.  Well?

Fred (*coming down* C *to* L *of the pram*)  Isn't it wonderful! You know what's happened, don't you?

Joe.  Yes. You've gone cracked!

Fred.  Nothing of the sort! It's a gift from the gods—this is!

Joe.  What is?

Fred.  The pram! Don't you see what it means?

Joe.  No!

Fred.  Look! You agree it's identical with the one we brought home the other night?

(Joe *nods*)

And we daren't explain how that pram got here?

(Joe *nods*)

Well—if we can find a satisfactory reason—everybody's in the clear—you—me—Cissie—Peter—all of us!

Joe.  I still don't get it.

Fred.  Then listen. The next time Gladys comes in here—you'll be down on your hands and knees repairing that wheel.

Joe.  But there's nothing wrong with it?

Fred (*shouting angrily*)  I know there isn't! (*He calms down with an effort*) You'll *pretend* to be mending it! Then—when Mrs Watson comes back, she'll thank you for doing the job; and you'll say: "I'm sorry, Mrs Watson, that it wasn't right the first time". Do you get that? "I'm sorry it wasn't right the first time!"

JOE.  But she hasn't been before?

FRED (*shouting angrily*)  *I know she hasn't!* (*He calms down again*) But you'll make it *appear* she has! She won't know what you're talking about—and when she's gone—we'll tell Gladys and Emma that that was why the pram was here last Saturday. *Now* —do you see?

JOE (*dubiously*)  Yes? It's clever—if it works!

FRED.  Of course it'll work! (*He moves the pram so that it is just* L *of* C *with the hood end pointing down* L) Now have you got some tools? (*He moves down* R)

JOE.  They're in there—(*indicating the door* R)—and the door's locked.

FRED.  Aren't there some anywhere else?

JOE.  There's a saw and an axe in the shed?

FRED (*irately*)  We're supposed to be mending it—not wrecking it! Wait a minute! There's a small hammer in the top drawer there. (*Pointing to the sideboard*) Have a look!

(JOE *rises, moves below the settee to the sideboard, opens the drawer, and takes out a hammer*)

Have you got it? Good! Now listen to me. When . . .

(*A door slam is heard off*)

Look out—they're coming back! Down on your knees and get to work!

(JOE *rushes to the pram, sits down in front of it, and starts hammering at the hub.*
     *The door* L *opens and* CISSIE *enters followed by* PETER. JOE *stops knocking.* PETER *remains up* L. CISSIE *comes down* L *to the sideboard*)

I thought I told you two . . . ?

CISSIE.  Sorry, Dad—I forgot my handbag. Ah—here it is! (*She points to it on the sideboard*)

(PETER *moves up to the window.* JOE *starts hammering again*)

Uncle Joe! What on earth are you doing? (*She moves upstage of the pram*)

JOE.  Mending the wheel.

CISSIE.  What—with the baby inside? Hammering like that? Of all the daft things! (*She bends over the pram and lifts out the baby, fondling it in her arms*)

(*The key rattles in the lock of the door* R)

(*Moving down* L *in front of the settee*) Never mind, there! Did the naughty man bang? Did he? (*She moves up* L)

FRED (*realizing the danger; moving down* R)  No, no! Cissie! *Put it down—quick!*

(CISSIE *ignores this. She is now at the upstage end of the settee.* JOE *rises and moves below the settee to the sideboard to replace the hammer. The door* R *opens and* EMMA *enters*)

EMMA (*moving* R *of the armchair*)  What's all the noise about? What's going on? (*She stops short catching sight of Cissie*) Cissie!

(GLADYS *enters from the kitchen* R)

GLADYS (*moving above the armchair to the front of it*)  Cissie— where? Cissie, love—why did you . . . ? (*She suddenly sees the pram— and then the child in Cissie's arms. Her reaction is swift*) Oh—no! It can't be! It can't be! Oh, Emma! (*She collapses in tears in the armchair*)

(EMMA *kneels beside her comforting her.* CISSIE *puts the baby back in the pram and sits on the upstage end of the settee.*

MRS WATSON *enters* L *coming down* C *to* L *of the pram. She carries a brown paper bag*)

MRS WATSON (*opening the bag and producing a hat*)  That's what I got, see! Isn't it a beauty?

(JOE *moves below the settee to the downstage end*)

(*To Joe*) I could kiss you—really I could!

JOE (*blindly following his instructions*)  Could you? Well, I think you'll find it better than the last time!

EMMA (*turning round*)  What!

FRED.  No—you fool! It's no use now. The whole thing's ruined!

JOE (*miserably*)  What are we going to do? (*He sits on the down-stage end of the settee*)

FRED.  The only thing we can do! Clear these youngsters! Listen, Gladys!

(GLADYS *gives way to a fresh burst of sobs*)

No—if you want the truth you've got to listen!

(GLADYS *subsides a little*)

That's better! Now, Mrs Watson—(*he points to the pram*)—has that anything to do with these two?

(PETER *joins Cissie behind the upstage end of the settee.* FRED *indicates them to Mrs Watson*)

MRS WATSON (*turning*)  With them? (*Decidedly*) Certainly not! That's mine—that is!

FRED (*to Gladys*)  There you are—see!

MRS WATSON.  I don't see how anybody could imagine they had! As a matter of fact—(*pointing to the pram*)—I've only got one person to thank for that!

FRED.  Who?

MRS WATSON.  Well—I'm not sure. It's either you—(*pointing to Fred*)—or him! (*She points to Joe*)

(GLADYS *goes off into hysterics.* EMMA *joins her in a quieter sort of way*)

FRED (*furiously; to Mrs Watson*)  Get that thing out of here at once!

(MRS WATSON *turns the pram and makes towards the door* L. *She stops* L *of the table and speaks as* GLADYS *quietens a little*)

MRS WATSON.  By the way—thanks for the money. I didn't spend it all—so I'll see Clarence has something out of it. Something that'll remind him of you—*both!*

(GLADYS *and* EMMA *let out another yell*)

Oh! And don't forget—you still owe me four days' sickness benefit! Toodle-oo!

(MRS WATSON *exits* L.

GLADYS *rises and rushes off upstairs* R, *alone.* EMMA *rises and turns up* R, *watching her go*)

FRED (*rushing after Gladys*)  Gladys! I can explain everything! Gladys! Come back! *Gladys!*

(FRED *disappears up the stairs after Gladys.* EMMA, *dabbing her eyes with her handkerchief, moves up* R *to the table and picks up the vase of flowers*)

PETER (*coming up* L *to her assistance*)  Mrs Derbyshire! Can I help you?

EMMA.  You can! (*Removing the flowers and handing them to Peter*) Take these out of here! (*She moves towards the stairs* R)

PETER.  What shall I do with them?

EMMA (*turning at the top of the stairs*)  Do with them? Stick them in the dustbin!

(*Breaking into tearful crying,* EMMA *disappears up the stairs*)

CISSIE (*sitting on the upstage arm of the settee; to Joe*)  You've made a fine mess of things, haven't you?

JOE (*still sitting on the settee, chin on his fists, staring miserably*)  Not *me*, Cissie. Your father! He's the master-mind!

PETER (*still holding the flowers, he has come down to* R *of Cissie*) He'll need to be superman as well—to get out of this lot!

CISSIE (*to Peter*)  Anyway—we're all right. We'll be able to have that white wedding after all.

JOE.  You're forgetting something.

PETER.  What?

JOE.  *Your* father.

PETER.  Oh, you needn't worry about that—mum's fixed him.

JOE.  How?

PETER.  She's made him promise that if she gets us back—he'll agree to the wedding.

JOE.  But she hasn't got you back?

PETER.  She will have—in five minutes! Come on, Cissie! (*He moves over to the door* L *still carrying the flowers*)

(CISSIE *rises, makes to move* C *then turns to* JOE)

CISSIE.  And you might tell everybody we're making another call on the way.

JOE (*rising*)  Where?

CISSIE.  At the vicar's. We're putting up the banns! Won't you wish us luck, Uncle Joe?

JOE.  That I will, love!

(CISSIE *moves down* L *to* JOE *and he kisses her*)

Now—off you go!

(CISSIE *goes towards the door* L *where Peter is waiting.* JOE *calls after her*)

And while you're about it—we could do with somebody calling round here!

CISSIE (*up* L)  The vicar?

JOE (*turning down* L)  The probation officer!

(CISSIE *laughs, and she and* PETER *disappear through the door* L.
FRED *enters disconsolately from the stairs and moves down* C.
JOE *returns to sit on the downstage end of the settee*)

JOE (*as he sits*)  Still not speaking?

FRED.  Oh, she's speaking all right!

JOE.  What did she say?

FRED.  Two things: "Bluebeard!" and "Mormon!" Never mind, I'll soon get us out of it!

JOE (*shaking his head*)  It's a funny thing—but every time you say that—somebody shoves us a bit deeper in!

FRED.  Are you suggesting *I'm* to blame?

JOE.  Shall we say—you're unlucky!

FRED (*sitting in the armchair* R)  So I'm a Jonah—am I?

JOE (*nodding agreement*)  Except for one thing. He only had *one* whale—you'd want a *school!*

FRED.  What for?

JOE.  To swallow your fancy ideas!

FRED.  Look here! If you think I'm going to . . .

(*The door* L *opens and* WILLIE WATSON'S *head peeps round*)

WILLIE.  Hey—Mr Furnival! Any more ice-cream?

(FRED *rises angrily, picks up the cushion from the armchair and hurls it at Willie's head.* WILLIE *closes the door hurriedly as the cushion bangs against it*)

FRED (*moving quickly above the settee to the sideboard*)  Joe! Do me a favour, will you? If ever he shows his nose in here again . . .

JOE.  Yes?

FRED (*picking up a sporting gun and displaying it above the settee*)  Put this where I can't find it! (*Having displayed it,* FRED *replaces the gun*)

JOE.  I understand how you feel. But don't be hasty! We're in enough trouble already.

FRED (*miserably*)  Trouble? (*Moving above the settee to down* C)  You don't know the half! (*Moving to the armchair* R)

JOE.  Is there something else?

FRED (*sitting in the armchair*)  We've lost the Cross-Channel Race!

JOE.  Lost it?

FRED.  Charlie Gibbs has just told me. Three birds are home. Bert Jones', Tom Mellor's, and, worst of all—his Smokey. It was clocked in two and a half hours ago. To think Charlie Gibbs has won—and our Sky hasn't come back! She's missing—she must be!

JOE.  But surely I told you?

FRED.  Told me what?

JOE.  No—I can't have done! Ah well—it's all this carry-on, you see, that's made me forget!

FRED.  What are you blathering about?

JOE.  The race. We haven't lost it—we've won it!

FRED (*rising*)  *Won* it?

JOE.  If what you say about those other birds is right. You see— Sky *is* back!

FRED (*almost shouting*)  *What!*

JOE (*rising*)  She's back! She came in—oh, four hours ago! Just before I went to the park.

FRED (*delighted*)  Four hours ago! Joe—I forgive you for everything! (*He makes to move down* R)  This makes up for the lot! (*He turns suddenly to Joe; apprehensive*)  Wait a minute! You clocked her in? You didn't forget that as well?

JOE (*calmly*)  Oh, no—(*he moves towards Fred*)—I remembered! I did it just like you showed me. I took the ring and put it in the clock!

(FRED *takes Joe by the arms and swings him round in a circle, one and a half times, so that* JOE *ends up on the* R *of Fred*)

JOE. Here! Steady on! Steady!

FRED (*stopping suddenly*) Joe! I could kiss you!

JOE (*taking a step back*) Now, now. Restrain yourself! There's no need to get nasty.

FRED. Nasty? I never felt better-tempered in my life! Where is it? Come on—*where* is it?

JOE. What?

FRED. The clock.

JOE (*pointing to the sideboard*) On there!

FRED (*moving above the settee to the sideboard*) Come to daddy! Oh, you beautiful thing! (*He kisses the clock*)

JOE. That's right! Get that out of your system!

FRED. Well—there's no time to lose. This must go to the secretary right away.

JOE. Can I take it?

FRED. Certainly not! You've done your good deed. It's my turn now.

JOE. All the same—I wish you'd let me do something.

FRED. Why?

JOE (*glancing towards the stairs*) I don't fancy stopping here!

FRED. All right. You go round to *The Bull*, and see how those eggs are getting on.

JOE. Fred—you're a pal!

FRED. Come on then.

(JOE *moves up to the door* L)

Because I want to see how . . .

(CHARLIE GIBBS *enters* L, *carrying a wallpaper pattern book, pushes past Joe and comes* L *of the table*)

CHARLIE (*to Fred*) I've got some news for you. (*Moving down* C)

(JOE *picks up the cushion which was flung at Willie*)

FRED (*behind the settee*) Really?

CHARLIE. That lad o' mine's back!

FRED. And I've got some news for you. That bird o' mine's back!

CHARLIE. Sky? Well—I'm glad. I don't like to hear of anybody losing a bird—not even you! It's a pity she wasn't a bit faster, though. Perhaps if she'd tagged along behind Smokey . . . ?

FRED *Behind* Smokey? She was that far in front—he couldn't see her tail-feathers for dust!

CHARLIE. Are you trying to say she's licked my bird?

FRED. Licked him? She kissed him good-bye before they left the French coast!

CHARLIE. But you said . . . ?

FRED. Never mind what *I* said! Ninety minutes to the good—

that's what *she* is! (*Holding up the clock*) She was clocked in four hours ago!

CHARLIE. Who by?

FRED (*pointing to Joe*) Him!

JOE (*advancing to the settee, jauntily and dropping the cushion on it*) The little lap-dog!

FRED. And he *forgot* to tell me! Isn't that rich? He forgot to *tell* me! Anyway, you stop and have a good laugh about it. I've got an appointment with the club secretary. Come on, Joe!

(JOE *exits* L *leaving the door open.* FRED *turns at the door for a parting shot*)

Oh, you might tell Gladys when she comes down. (*He points to the stairs*) And if I were you—I'd have a look at Smokey's feet. If they're dusty—he walked it!

(FRED *exits* L *with a peal of laughter, leaving the door open.* CHARLIE, *in disgust, flings the pattern book under the table.* WILLIE WATSON *enters* L, *closing the door behind him*)

WILLIE. Oh, you're there? (*He moves to the upstage end of the settee*) I wondered where you'd got to.

CHARLIE. Yes—and I've been wondering where *you'd* got to! Where've you been these last four days?

WILLIE. Sick! I've been proper poorly—I have!

CHARLIE. And now you've come back—is that it?

WILLIE. No. I've come to ask for another day off.

CHARLIE (*sarcastically*) Really! Will that be enough?

WILLIE. Oh, no! I want a rise as well!

CHARLIE. A rise?

WILLIE. Ten shillings a week—that's what my mam says. And if I don't get it—you know what!

CHARLIE. I'm afraid I don't. What am I supposed to know?

WILLIE. I've got a big mouth—I have!

CHARLIE. Yes—and you've got a big head, too! Come here!

(WILLIE *moves down* C *to* CHARLIE, *who seizes him by the ear*)

WILLIE. *Ow!*

CHARLIE. So you want a day off—*and* ten shillings a week rise?

WILLIE. That's right.

CHARLIE. And maybe next week—you'd like *two* days off— and a *pound* rise?

WILLIE. I haven't said . . .

CHARLIE. No—but you would! Well, listen to me, my lad. You've milked this coconut for the last time!

WILLIE. What do you mean?

CHARLIE. I'll show you! (*He leads* WILLIE *over to the foot of the stairs, still holding him by the ear and calls*) Gladys!

GLADYS (*off,* R) Yes?

CHARLIE. Come down here, will you? And if Emma's there—
bring her, too!

(CHARLIE *returns* C *still dragging Willie by the ear.*
GLADYS *enters from the stairs, followed by* EMMA. GLADYS
*moves in front of the armchair* R *and* EMMA *stays above the fireplace*)

GLADYS. Now what's the matter?
CHARLIE. I want you to hear something.
GLADYS. If it's about Fred—I've heard *everything!*
CHARLIE. I don't think so. There's still a lot you don't know.
EMMA. What did I tell you? I said *she* wouldn't be the only
one!
GLADYS (*to Charlie*) Is Joe in this as well?
CHARLIE. Partly. But he only does what he's told.
GLADYS. And I'll bet he doesn't need much telling! Well—who
are they?
CHARLIE (*puzzled*) Who are who?
EMMA. These other women!
CHARLIE. Wait a minute. There must be a misunderstanding.
There aren't any women in this—except you two!
GLADYS. Why don't you say what you want to say?
CHARLIE. I'm trying to—but you won't let me!
WILLIE. Mr Gibbs!
CHARLIE. Well?
WILLIE. Change ears! That's going numb!
CHARLIE. Shut up!

(CHARLIE *releases Willie's ear.* WILLIE *goes down* L)

Listen, Gladys—you know the mess this lad made for you?
GLADYS. Yes?
CHARLIE. Well, he didn't!
GLADYS. I see—it was a mirage?
CHARLIE. No! I mean *he* didn't do it. It was Fred! Ask her—
she knows. (*Pointing to Emma*)
EMMA. That's right. They were both drunk.
GLADYS (*sitting in the armchair* R) But why should this lad
say . . . ?
CHARLIE. Because Fred bribed him. And now the young
monkey's trying to put the screws on me!
GLADYS. But you sacked him!
CHARLIE. I pretended to.
GLADYS. Why?
CHARLIE. Because Fred bribed *me!*
GLADYS. I'm beginning to think it's a pity Fred isn't in politics.
In South America he'd probably end up as president! (*Pointing
to Willie*) So you didn't sack him?
CHARLIE. No! But I'm going to remedy that right now. Willie!
WILLIE. Yes?

F

CHARLIE. Go back to the shop and get your cards!

WILLIE. But—Mr Gibbs . . . ?

CHARLIE (*turning him around by the shoulders and kicking Willie's behind*) And this time you really get 'em!

(WILLIE *runs blubbering towards the door* L)

WILLIE (*turning up* L) You wait till my mam knows!

CHARLIE (*raising his arm threateningly*) Gertcher!

(WILLIE *exits* L, *still blubbering*)

GLADYS (*to Charlie*) And that puts everything right?

CHARLIE. Not quite. There's still something neither of you know. When those two got drunk—they came home on an ice-cream thingumybob!

EMMA. Both of them?

CHARLIE. Only Fred! Joe was in the other.

GLADYS. And was that a pram?

CHARLIE (*surprised*) So you weren't in the dark?

GLADYS. I was—but daylight's peeping through! After that—they did the decorating, I suppose.

CHARLIE. Only Fred! Joe went to work.

EMMA. He never told me.

CHARLIE. So you didn't hear about the burglary?

EMMA. What burglary?

CHARLIE. Joe saw some chaps breaking into the warehouse. He gave the alarm—and the boss gave him a pound a week rise!

EMMA. Well—of all the deceitful . . . !

GLADYS. I shouldn't be too hard on Joe, Emma. It's the man at the top we're after, and I don't think he'll be hard to find!

(FRED'S *voice is heard approaching* L, *singing jubilantly*)

EMMA. He's coming now—like a Russian nightingale!

GLADYS. When I've finished—he'll be more like Florence Nightingale!

CHARLIE (*moving towards the door* L) I'd better go.

GLADYS. Not you! We may need you—sit down! (*Indicating the pouffe down* R)

(CHARLIE *goes and sits down* R.
FRED *enters happily through the door* L, *still singing. He carries the same bunch of flowers he brought in previously*)

FRED (*stopping his song and moving* C *above the table*) Well, well, the reception committee! (*Pointing to the flowers*) Oh! I found these in the dustbin. (*He starts putting the flowers back in the vase on the table, as he sings to the tune of "Granada"*)

> Old Smokey got lost,
> And was left far behind in
> Granada.

GLADYS (*interrupting*) Hey—Carl Rosa!

(FRED *stops*)

Listen to me!

FRED (*putting his hand up*) No, no! You listen to me! There's been one or two misunderstandings around here—and it's time they were cleared up. Charlie here thought I wasn't going to race my pigeon. *That* was a misunderstanding! Then there was that business the other night. Well! I had a dream, and . . .

GLADYS. Wait a minute! I've had a dream, too! I dreamt that you came home on an ice-cream cart—with a pram for company! And when you got in—you had a misunderstanding with some wallpaper and a bucket!

FRED. I see. (*Moving R of the table to Charlie*) You've split, eh? (*Snapping his fingers at Charlie*) Well, if you hadn't told 'em—I was going to! I don't care what happens—I'm much too excited over Sky's win!

(JOE *enters* L, *followed by* JIM DOBSON, *who is in mufti, evidently now off duty.* JIM *carries a large carpet bag.* JOE *moves down* L *behind the settee.* JIM *moves to the* L *corner of the table*)

(*Seeing them*) Well, well! It never rains but it pours! (*Moving to Jim*) Well, what is it this time? More obstruction with the bike?

JIM. That's quite enough of that! I've called because I've got some news.

FRED. Good news?

JIM. Some! And some's not so good! You remember buying a draw ticket?

FRED. A ticket? You soaked us for four books!

JIM. Well—I'm happy to tell you you've won the first prize!

FRED (*elated*) Do you hear that, Joe? Everything's coming home at once!

JOE. I don't like to mention it, Fred—but you haven't paid me for those tickets.

FRED. I'm surprised at you! Anyway, I'll show you the kind of man I am. Half of that prize is yours! Do you hear?

JOE. Thanks very much.

FRED. And that reminds me. We were talking about dreams. Well—I've had another dream. (*Turning to Gladys*) Gladys!

GLADYS. Yes?

FRED. I had a lovely dream just now. I dreamt I saw you in a new winter coat!

GLADYS. Did you?

FRED. I did and all! Joe!

JOE. Yes?

FRED. Give her ten pounds!

JOE. *What?*

FRED. Give her ten pounds! I'll refund it when we get the prize money. (*He moves to Joe*)

(JOE *extracts some money from his wallet*)

JIM. I think I ought to mention . . .

FRED (*taking the money from Joe; to Jim*) Be quiet! (*He crosses to Gladys and hands her the money*) How dare you interrupt such a beautiful dream!

EMMA. And what about me?

FRED. You?

EMMA. You aren't the only one that has dreams! I dreamt I saw Joe going to work, and he did some brave deed. I couldn't quite see what it was—but I distinctly saw the boss giving him a rise! (*Pondering*) Now was it twenty-five shillings?

JOE. It's a lie! It was only . . . (*His hand flies to his mouth; suddenly realizing his mistake*)

EMMA. And then the scene changed. I was inside a big store with Gladys. We were both trying on winter coats!

FRED. Joe! You know that half share you've just won?

JOE. Yes?

FRED. You've lost it!

JOE. But I've not drawn!

FRED. Neither have I. (*Crossing L to Joe*) And I didn't make a fuss. Come on—shell out! (*He grabs the money from Joe, and crosses back R to Emma, giving it to her*) There we are, see. Everybody's happy!

JIM. I still think . . . !

FRED (*moving C in front of the table*) Except the limb of the law! And what sort of a rake-off are you expecting?

JIM. If I had my uniform on—I'd resent that! But I've still got something you ought to hear.

FRED. Oh, yes—the other news. What is it?

JIM. On my way here, I called at the pigeon club.

FRED. And you heard the news? By the way—your money's on! Big Sam laid me "three's".

JIM. That's what's worrying me.

FRED. I ought to have got a better price?

JIM. You ought to have got a better ring!

FRED. What do you mean—"a better ring"?

JIM. That ring in your clock. The club secretary says it isn't the one they put on Sky's leg before the race!

CHARLIE (*rising*) What!

FRED (*trying to grasp it*) It isn't *what?*

JIM. It's not the ring that was issued for the race!

FRED (*turning on Joe*) I thought you told me you'd put that ring in the clock as soon as Sky arrived?

JOE. So I did! As soon as I saw it circle around and settle.

FRED. Did you get it off Sky's leg?

Joe. Should I have done? You never said! All you said was: "As soon as Sky comes in, get the ring and put it in the clock!"

Fred (*ominously*)  And where did you get the ring from?

Joe. Out of the bag. You know—the one you showed me how to do it with.

Fred (*furiously*)  You dunder-headed old fool! You knew it had to be the one off the pigeon's leg?

Joe. You didn't say! In any case—I *couldn't* have got it off Sky's leg.

Fred. Why not?

Joe. She hasn't come down yet. She's still on top of the roof with that seagull!

Fred (*almost dancing with rage*)  You fathead! Don't you realize what's happened?

Charlie (*laughing*)  *I* do! My Smokey's won the race!

Fred (*crossing* L *of Jim towards Joe*)  Get out of my house! D'you hear me? Get out—and never let me see your face again!

Joe. But, Fred—I . . .

Fred. Go on—disappear—vamoosh—scarper!

(Joe *moves below the settee to the sideboard, picks up his bowler, and moves to the door* L)

Joe. All right. If that's the way you feel—good-bye!

(Joe *turns, and exits sadly* L)

Jim. Never mind, Fred. It isn't all bad. There's still the draw.

Fred. That's right—the twenty quid! (*Coming back down* C) When will you be paying out?

Jim. That's what I was trying to tell you. There is none!

Fred. No pay out? But you'll have to! It's on the tickets—first prize—twenty pounds.

Jim. First prize—*value* twenty pounds!

Fred. So that's a swizzle as well! All right—what is it?

Jim (*picking up and opening his carpet bag*)  Something any housewife will be glad to have!

Fred. I can't wait to hear. Go on—astonish me!

Jim (*taking out a stack of rolls of wallpaper*)  The first prize is to have one of your rooms completely decorated. Charlie here to do the job—the lucky winner to pick his own paper! (*Unrolling one of the rolls of wallpaper*)  Now—how would you like that?

(*The pattern of the paper is once again identical with that on the walls of the room. For a moment* Fred *is transfixed. Then he seizes the roll of paper from* Jim, *and taking it in both hands, brings it down over the astonished policeman's head.* Jim *collapses in the chair* L *of the table.* Charlie Gibbs *points at* Jim *and doubles up with laughter, turning away down* R. Fred *looks at him, then, very purposefully, he picks up another roll of the paper and begins to unroll it.* Charlie *is taking no notice.* FRED *comes up behind him, and as* CHARLIE *straightens up from one of his paroxysms of laughter,* FRED *claps the paper down over his head, so that like Jim, his head sticks through and it drapes down over his shoulders. This effectively silences* CHARLIE. *At the same time, the irate voice of* MRS WATSON *is heard off* L)

MRS WATSON (*off* L) Where is he? Just let me get at him! I'll settle this!

(MRS WATSON *enters through the door* L *like a ship in full sail.* WILLIE, *rubbing his eyes, stands in the doorway.* FRED *has already picked up another roll of paper, and has it ready in his hands*)

MRS WATSON (*moving down* C *faces Charlie*) Oh—there you are! Now what's all this 'ere about our Willie? *You* can't sack him!
FRED. Hey! Just a minute!
MRS WATSON (*turning to him*) Well?
FRED. Come here!

(MRS WATSON *moves towards him. As soon as she gets near enough,* FRED *lifts the roll and brings it down over her head in the same manner*)

MRS WATSON. Well—of all the . . . (*She collapses* C *of the settee*)

(WILLIE, *who is framed in the doorway* L, *is suddenly moved aside. The pathetic figure of* JOE *enters.* JOE *moves down* C, L *of Fred.* FRED *takes up another roll of paper and advances a step towards Joe*)

FRED. I thought I told you never to show your face in here again?
JOE. I'm sorry—but I just had to come back! It's about the other pigeon.
FRED. What other pigeon?
JOE. The one at *The Bull*. It's hatched out Sky's eggs!
FRED (*dropping the roll*) Glory be!

(JOE *moves down* L)

(*To Charlie*) D'you hear that? I may have lost the race—but I've got some new cross-Channel champions! Two of 'em!
JOE. I don't think they will be—unless they swim it!
FRED. Swim it! What are you talking about?
JOE. Well—you see—they've got webbed feet!
FRED. *Webbed feet?* (*Realization suddenly dawning*) That sea-gull!

(FRED *rushes over to the sideboard, picks up the gun, and comes back* L *of the table checking it*)

JIM. Hey! Have you got a licence for that thing?
FRED. I've got a death warrant for it!

(PETER, CISSIE *and the* CURATE *enter* L.
FRED *pushes his way through them and disappears* L. WILLIE

*moves* L *of the window.* CISSIE *crosses excitedly behind the table to Gladys)*

CISSIE. Mum! We've put up the banns! We're getting married!
GLADYS. Well—if you're happy, love—I'm happy for you!
CISSIE. Thanks! We brought the curate along in case anything wants smoothing over.
CURATE. How do you do, Mrs Furnival? I hope everything's going to be all right. (*He stands above the settee, on Jim's* R)
GLADYS. So do I!

(*A shot rings out off stage* L)

JIM. Well—I'm sorry—but if he's not got a gun licence—there's going to be trouble!

(FRED *re-enters, carrying the gun. He goes over to the sideboard and replaces it, then comes down* C)

Well?
FRED. Justice has been done! (*He stoops to pick up a roll of wallpaper*)
CISSIE (*moving up* R *to the corner of the table*) Dad! We're being married on the twenty-first of next month! Isn't it wonderful?
FRED (*disinterestedly*) Marvellous!
CURATE (*moving above the settee towards Fred*) By the way, Mr Furnival—I hear your bird was back first again! She's a wonder, that Sky, isn't she?
FRED (*turning to him with the paper in his hands*) Sky? A wonder? (*Bringing down the roll over the Curate's head*) She's the bloody limit!

FRED *stalks out* L *as*—

*the* CURTAIN *falls*

*When the* CURTAIN *rises again the* CURATE *is lying back on the settee being revived by* GLADYS *with a glass of water,* JIM DOBSON *is by the sideboard examining the gun;* CHARLIE, MRS WATSON *and* WILLIE *are arguing by the door* L *and* FRED *is seen outside the box-window persuading Sky to come down.* CISSIE *and* PETER *are* R *of the window watching Fred and* JOE *is pleading with Emma by the armchair* R *as*—

*the* CURTAIN *falls for the second time*

# ALTERNATIVE ENDING

CURATE. How do you do, Mrs Furnival? I hope everything's going to be all right. (*He stands above the settee, on Jim's* R)

GLADYS. So do I!

(*A shot rings off* L)

JIM. Well—I'm sorry—but if he's not got a gun licence—there's going to be trouble!

(FRED *enters* L *carrying the gun. He goes to the sideboard and replaces it then moves down* C)

Well?

FRED. Justice has been done! (*He stoops to pick up a roll of wall-paper*)

CISSIE (*moving up* R *to the corner of the table*) Dad! We're being married on the twenty-first of next month! Isn't it wonderful?

FRED (*disinterestedly*) Marvellous! (*To Gladys*) By the way— what's for dinner tomorrow?

GLADYS. I haven't christened it yet!

FRED. Well, I have! We're having that bird!

GLADYS. What—seagull?

FRED. No—pigeon pie! I've shot the wrong one!

*Turning to the Curate* FRED *slaps the roll of wallpaper down on his head and then he stalks off* L *as—*


*the* CURTAIN *falls*


*When the* CURTAIN *rises again the scene is the same as in the first ending except that* FRED *is shaking his fist at the seagull instead of persuading Sky to come down.*

# PRODUCTION NOTES

The Ground Plan indicates how the setting is changed between Acts II and III by reversing a number of flats on the R of the stage. The half-flat containing the kitchen door R is obviously not reversible as this would make the door open in the opposite direction in Act III. This difficulty can be overcome by having another half-flat ready with the new wallpaper above the door or alternatively the same flat can be kept merely by stapling a piece of the new wallpaper above the door up to the border.

The ice-cream bicycle is easily adapted from an ordinary tradesman's bicycle with a front carrier basket, by building a cardboard box-like structure around the basket, complete with lid. The name "Tornelli" must be painted on the plate which is usually incorporated in the centre of the frame.

Between Acts I and II the crazy wallpapering is easily achieved by using an ordinary hinged office stapling machine and pinning the lengths to the flats.

In the Seven Veils sequence in Act I the six lengths of wallpaper (about 5 feet long) should have two reinforcing strips gummed along the outer edges. A cross-cut in the centre of each will ensure that Emma's head protrudes through at the right place. The six lengths should be laid evenly along the pasting-board, so that Fred can transport them easily to Emma. Fred should contrive to bring Emma's head through them so that they hang down fore and aft, then Emma can easily rip them off one at a time in the shedding process.

The rolls used at the end of Act III should be similarly treated, that is, reinforced at the outer edges and cross-cuts made for heads to go through.

# FURNITURE AND PROPERTY LIST

*NOTE:* Flats A, B, D and E are reversible, old wallpaper on one side and new on the other. The other flats are papered with the new wallpaper. Flat C, if a reserve flat is not being used, should have a new strip of wallpaper stapled above the door up to the border during the second interval.

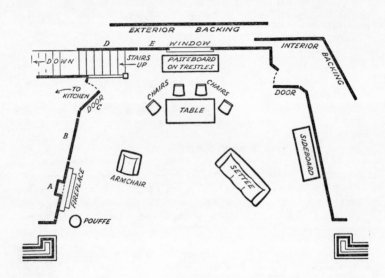

## ACT I

*On stage:*   Paste-board on trestles. *On it:* cut lengths of wallpaper and loose rolls

Gate-leg table

4 bentwood chairs

Sideboard. *On it:* pipe (CHARLIE), knitting, electric torch (EMMA), bowler hat (JOE). *In cupboard:* bottle of Arrack and 3 tumblers. *In drawer:* clothes

Pouffe

Armchair. *On it:* jacket (CHARLIE)

Settee

Painter's ladders (*labelled:* C. GIBBS, DECORATOR) *On them:* paste bucket

Stag's head (*above fireplace*)

Slippers (*in hearth*) (FRED)
Dust sheets on furniture

*Off stage:*   Parcels, tray, teapot, cups, 2 plates of baked beans on toast,
salt, cutlery, evening paper, thermos flask, packet of sand-
wiches, wicker basket. *In it:* milk bottles (EMMA)
Tea-tray, cup and saucer, etc. (GLADYS)
Bicycle with bell, parcel of wallpaper, pigeon basket, live
pigeon (FRED)
Bicycle pump (JOE)
Book of draw tickets (JIM)
Suitcase (CISSIE)

*Personal:*   WILLIE: comic
JOE: pipe, ten-shilling note
JIM: notebook
EMMA: handkerchief

# ACT II

*Scene:*   The same
*Set:*   Strips of wallpaper over box-window, door L and criss-crossed over
walls on R half of set (*as instructed in the Production Notes and the
description of the set*)
Pile of wallpaper on settee (*to hide* FRED)
*On sideboard:* pen and pad (FRED), pigeon basket
*On table:* jacket (FRED)

*Off stage:*   Roughly folded sheets (CISSIE)
Pigeon clock (JOE)
2 ice-cream blocks (WILLIE)
Towel, shaving brush and pot (FRED)
Fred's bicycle
Ice-cream bicycle
Pram

*Personal:*   FRED: handkerchief, 2 half-crowns, ten-shilling note

# ACT III

*Strike:*   Wallpaper and painter's equipment
Reverse flats A, B, D, E to give a uniform look to set
Staple new wallpaper over flat C (*if substitute is not used*)

*Set:*  Cushion in armchair
*On table:* cutlery, cruet, cloth, mats, glasses, plates. *On them:* chops
         vegetables; mint sauce boat
*On sideboard:* empty cut glass vase, pigeon clock. *In drawer:* small
         hammer
Sporting rifle *(behind upstage end of sideboard)*

*Off stage:*  2 bunches of flowers all same colour *(to be identical)* (FRED)
         Plate. *On it:* beans on toast (EMMA)
         Plate. *On it:* beans on toast (GLADYS)
         Pram. *In it:* dummy baby; brown paper bag. *In it:* hat (MRS
         WATSON)
         Wallpaper pattern book (CHARLIE)
         Carpet bag. *In it:* rolls of wallpaper (JIM)

*Personal:*  CISSIE: handbag
         CHARLIE: envelope
         EMMA: handkerchief
         JOE: twenty one-pound notes

# LIGHTING PLOT

Property fittings required: central pendant (practical)
> Interior. A living-room. The same scene throughout
>> THE MAIN ACTING AREAS are at an armchair R, by a table C, by a door L and at a settee L
>> THE APPARENT SOURCES OF LIGHT are in daytime, a box-window C and at night a central pendant light

ACT I.  Friday night

Effect of dusk
Central fitting on
Strips outside doors R and L

| *Cue* 1 | EMMA: ". . . you nasty thing" | (Page 24) |
| | *She re-enters, takes up torch and switches off light* | |
| | *Snap out pendant* | |
| | | |
| *Cue* 2 | CISSIE: ". . . the milk bottles?" | (Page 24) |
| | CISSIE *switches on the light* | |
| | *Snap in pendant* | |
| | | |
| *Cue* 3 | CISSIE *picks up suitcase and switches off light* | (Page 26) |
| | *Snap out pendant* | |
| | | |
| *Cue* 4 | EMMA *enters* R *with torch, switches on light* | (Page 27) |
| | *Snap in pendant* | |

ACT II.  Early the following morning

Effect of sunlight
*No cues*

ACT III.  Lunchtime, the following Thursday

Effect of daylight
*No cues*

# EFFECTS PLOT

## ACT I

| | | |
|---|---|---|
| *Cue* 1 | FRED: ". . . for a naval officer!"<br>*Bicycle rings violently* | (Page 7) |
| *Cue* 2 | EMMA: ". . . he's here!"<br>*Sound of kicking on door* L | (Page 7) |
| *Cue* 3 | FRED: ". . . with this toast!"<br>*Loud knocking on front door* | (Page 18) |
| *Cue* 4 | FRED: ". . . off your stomach!"<br>*Knocking at door* L | (Page 21) |
| *Cue* 5 | JOE *sits on settee*<br>*Knocking is repeated* | (Page 21) |
| *Cue* 6 | *At rise of* CURTAIN<br>*Rattling at front door* | (Page 24) |
| *Cue* 7 | CISSIE *scuttles upstairs* R<br>*Crash followed by sound of milk bottles rolling about* | (Page 26) |
| *Cue* 8 | FRED: ". . . Right—*shove!*"<br>*A dull thud is heard* | (Page 26) |
| *Cue* 9 | FRED: ". . . Dawnsh breaking! Right—shove!"<br>*Clatter outside door* L | (Page 27) |

## ACT II

| | | |
|---|---|---|
| *Cue* 10 | EMMA: ". . . Gladys is bound to . . ."<br>*Loud knocking at front door* | (Page 34) |
| *Cue* 11 | FRED: ". . . fracturing my skull!"<br>*Knocking is repeated* | (Page 34) |
| *Cue* 12 | FRED: ". . . Off you go—quick!"<br>*Loud knocking at front door* | (Page 35) |
| *Cue* 13 | FRED: ". . . be your mother!"<br>*Knocking repeated urgently* | (Page 35) |
| *Cue* 14 | CISSIE *enters* R *carrying sheets*<br>*Knocking on door* R | (Page 46) |

## ACT III

*Cue* 15    JOE: ". . . I can't!"    (Page 62)
          *Banging on door* L

*Cue* 16    FRED: ". . . Now listen to me. When . . ."    (Page 70)
          *A door slams*

*Cue* 17    CISSIE: ". . . the daft things!"    (Page 70)
          *Key rattles in door* R

*Cue* 18    GLADYS: "So do I!"    (Page 83)
          *A shot rings out* L